Winning Client Trust

Winning Client Trust
The Retail Distribution Review and the UK financial services industry's battle for their clients' hearts and minds

First published in 2011 by
Ecademy Press
48 St Vincent Drive, St Albans, Herts, AL1 5SJ
info@ecademy-press.com
www.ecademy-press.com

Printed and Bound by Lightning Source in the UK and USA
Designed by Angela Ellis

Printed on acid-free paper from managed forests. This book is printed on demand, so no copies will be remaindered or pulped.

ISBN 978-1-907722-46-2

The right of Chris Davies to be identified as the author of this work has been inserted in accordance with sections 77 and 78 of the Copyright Designs and Patents Act 1988.

A CIP catalogue record for this book is available from the British Library.

This book is available online and all good bookstores.

Winning Client Trust

The Retail Distribution Review and the
UK financial services industry's battle for their
clients' hearts and minds

Chris Davies

To my amazing wife Saleema and our ever beautiful girls, Kaia and Teagan. Thank you for being my family and yes putting up with the 'fun and games' roller coaster this book-writing project has proven to be. Not forgetting Bella my running partner.

Contents

Acknowledgements

Firstly and foremostly a big thanks to Les Cantlay for his ever expansive bold thinking and thought contribution in my writing this book. I also need to make a special mention to my wife Saleema for the never-ending support and copy writing skills without which I would still be half way through the first draft!

Thanks to Matthew Harris for a keen copywriting eye and help in the first 8 chapters and also to Mindy Gibbins-Klein for facilitating an amazing coaching programme to provide a structure for a book writing process. I would also like to express sincere thanks to Andrew and Daniel Priestley for their respective super human business coaching programmes which have helped my career move into consultancy to be as smooth and as successful as possible.

I also thank Professor Rob Briner, David Ferguson, Greg Davies, Robert Bernard, Professor Merlin Stone, Mike Harris, Bryan Foss, David Lambert, TISA's Malcolm Small, Rikki Sorbie & Matthew Lamont (for making my photo shoots less painful) John Robinson of the Social Market Foundation, Pat Tuohy, Which? Magazine, JP Morgan, Citywire, Oxera and Capita Financial Software for all the relevant support in their respective valuable contributions.

Finally a thank you to all those inspirational characters out there who act with integrity and have made things happen despite the obstacles and challenges faced.

Preface

This book is a culmination of 20 years working within the financial services industry both in the UK and internationally. In my travels around UK, Europe, Middle East and Asia, I have found to my initial surprise, that the frustrations, challenges and opportunities faced by market participants are somehow similar and can be placed in three key relationship areas:

1. Regulatory directives
2. Industry pressures
3. Consumer needs

What seems to have frustrated me most in my career is the fact that although the 3 principles apply in general, it has never been easy to find relevant information in one repository or publication that could aid support in building a business or meeting change management challenges.

When it comes to winning client trust, there is no doubt that the 3rd area is the most important and financial organisations face the difficult task of spinning plates to sustain client loyalty between compliance with regulatory strategies and keeping ahead of industry pressures such as the competition and product or service design.

Yet with similar challenges, no one outcome can be predicted. Different cultures and organisational climates certainly play a strong part in this, yet what has become of great interest to me is the fact that it's the behavioural economics and the irrationality of human nature that also plays a distinguished role in augmenting all 3 of the above areas.

The fact that you can give two organisations the same resources and regulatory directives and they deliver different outcomes means nothing is straightforward. It is this issue that fascinates me where winning client trust is concerned. With the UK retail investment market facing the huge change directive called the Retail Distribution Review (RDR) we now see an interesting and exciting time where market participants will battle hard to gain their place at the RDR table post 2012. They now face a huge task in their fight for their client's trust and loyalty. So it is with relish that I write about my key findings and insights into the journey market participants are taking and will face through the regulators client protection agenda and how successful outcomes can be reached by application of some basic principles.

Note on reading this book

When starting this project I decided to attempt to create a 'repository' of information for the interested reader who maybe affected by some of the issues detailed.

I have placed what I call 'hanging boxes' within the text to give a more focused view on key issues and thus this will hopefully give the reader an easy reference to information if indeed they are involved within the financial services industry and affected by the regulatory changes or just plain interested.

Although there are many industry related issues, topics and regulatory directives cited, I would also hope the consumers of financial services may also be able to use the book as a reference tool to give guidance on the change the Retail Distribution Review brings in its industry re-pricing, professionalisation and client protection agenda.

A healthy debate is needed between all market participants (including the consumer) to ensure the journey to the RDR new world order is as smooth and understood as possible. I have therefore placed #RDRBOOK against areas that maybe of interest to those of us in the twitter fraternity which may help with issues for discussion, business development or client engagement when it comes to change management, progress made and client viewpoints on key areas and strategies.

Finally the book is also about the importance of psychology within business and in nurturing and maintaining client trust. I have leaned on behavioural economics and social science to produce strategies that can be employed to enable better capabilities for the industry and clients alike in their quest for a mutually rewarding relationship.

Testimonials

"Winning Client Trust explains exactly how to place the client at the heart of the financial services industry for the benefit of both businesses and customers".

Mike Harris, Chairman of Garlik and founder of three iconic brands - First Direct, Egg and Mercury One to One

"Chris is the man to watch through the significant changes ahead in financial advice & planning. He's looked forward into the future of the industry and found the path for delivering value, using cutting edge ideas and technology and getting rewarded. Those who bury their heads in the sand aren't just avoiding looking at the threats, they're missing the opportunity as well. Read Chris's book for a whole new perspective and a clear way to make your move forward."

Daniel Priestley, Founder of Triumphant Events and best selling author of "Key Person of Influence"

"A brilliant book which is packed full of common sense. Winning Client Trust helps you turn your business the right way up by focusing you on strategies to really make a difference. Chris truly knows his stuff and you'll find loads of tried and tested and proven ideas inside."

Lee Gilbert, The Serious Players' Webmaster and author of 'Turning Monkeys into Lemons'

"This book MUST be read by anyone with any involvement in marketing or selling more complex financial services products to consumers, or advising consumers about how to manage their long-term finances. Its comprehensive and deep analysis will help readers future-proof their companies, whether against market developments or regulatory attacks."

Professor Merlin Stone DPhil, FCIM, Hon FIDM, Professor of Marketing at Surrey European Management School and author of fourteen books on marketing and customer service.

"We welcome RDR, just as we welcome your work in pulling together this book."

David Ferguson, Managing Director Nucleus Wrap.

"A must-read for any IFA wishing to position their business to compete in the post-RDR world. Full of insightful research and sound advice, Davies combines a deep understanding of implications that RDR presents the industry, with clear thinking on managing the change process for both clients and employees."

Suresh Mistry Partner Korda and Partners consultancy and co-author of 'Leading strategy execution'.

"KISS was an acronym coined by Kelly Johnson, lead engineer at the famous Lockheed Skunk Works. Whilst today it translates as 'Keep it simple stupid', the principle is best illustrated by the story of Johnson handing a team of design engineers a handful of tools, with the challenge that the jet aircraft they were designing must be repairable by an average mechanic in the field under combat conditions with only these tools.

Hence, the 'stupid' refers to the relationship between the way things break and the sophistication available to fix them. Regulation should be more about foresight and less about hindsight. It should separate advice and product. This may be a simplistic view that is at least worth a discussion, but KISS seems a pretty relevant acronym to use for an RDR route map today. This book by Chris Davies addresses many of the challenges and fears both IFAs and the industry in general face and provides foresight to navigate through the perilous waters faced by all in the transition.

Derek Bradley CEO PanaceaIFA

"This book is the first to be published which takes a view of what the effects for UK consumers will be from implementation of the Retail Distribution Review. This Review will fundamentally alter the way in which financial advice is paid for and will engender massive change in the way that financial products and services are obtained. Some commentators have referred to it as the biggest reform in UK financial services for over a hundred years and its impending implementation is already changing the landscape for distribution of these products and services. Advisory firms and financial services providers alike will need to undertake change programmes of a substantial scale if they are to survive and be relevant and valued in this new landscape. The book's publication is therefore timely, studying as it does, through the lens of behavioural economics, the likely effects of the Review's implementation. It is a valuable contribution to the debate on the future form of retail financial services and advice provision in this country."

Malcolm Small Director of Policy Tax Incentivised Savings Association (TISA)

"Chris has taken a long, hard look at the behaviours exhibited by both investors and advisers, coming up with sound advice around the need to place clients at the center of any RDR adjustment strategy; and trust at the center of any client strategy."

David Lambert Managing Director of training consultancy IOWEU and co-author of 'Smart Selling'.

Winning Client Trust places the emphasis on the financial industry to embrace fundamental, systematic and necessary change to ensure clients needs are not only met but understood"

Justin Basini CEO and Founder ALLOW and author of "Why Should Anyone Buy from You?"

Introduction

"May you live in interesting times" Chinese proverb

We are certainly living in truly extraordinary times when it comes to consumerism. We may now purchase products with a mobile phone scan application, engage in all forms of communication, at any time, with individuals we have never and may never meet and are bombarded with products to buy, in some very clever ways, every minute of each day. The psychology of understanding the customer and his or her needs has therefore never been more important to business along with the consumers themselves ensuring their self defence mechanisms are up to scratch!

Such social dynamics means that business has to remain at the cutting edge of their chosen markets, whether this entails employing key persons of influence in their field, state-of-the-art technology or ensuring market intelligence is retained easily and quickly. For clients they need to be aware of their own motivations, behavioural tendencies and capabilities when it comes to financial planning and purchasing investment products. This all means that we begin to see an important relational exchange where nothing maybe assumed and lessons need to be learnt quickly in order to survive and win.

Never before has there been a time where public scrutiny has been so sharply focused on accountability of both the public and private sectors. Validation of business practice is essential and without this then client trust will be nothing but a pipe dream.

This book addresses one of the biggest regulatory challenges ever seen within UK industry; the Financial Services Authority's (FSA) Retail Distribution Review (RDR) customer protection agenda and the move from commission to fee remuneration for the UK retail financial services industry. The reasons why this directive is so wide ranging is it effectively re-prices an industry used to a certain way of operating for over 50 years. This along with organisational culture and regulatory climate change and the accompanying processes, is really unprecedented and all the major issues regarding the change management, business model re-structuring and the psychological impact of such radical mandatory adjustment are now playing out ten-fold for organisations impacted by the RDR.

In this book I address the issues that surround the RDR and the industries fight for their clients' support and loyalty. Firstly, commentating on the challenges as I see them, I aim to bed down some RDR 'myths and legends' that have appeared which continue to rattle and upset firms facing transition to the new world order. Next we take an in-depth look at how the industry has evolved towards the RDR and then, as seen from the customers' point of view, we investigate change processes, the business value chains and best possible ways organisations can place their clients' needs at the heart of their business models. We then take a view on how behavioural skills and behavioural economics, marketing and technology can facilitate productive and innovative business relations. Finally I provide a seven-point action plan to pull together the main issues discussed.

The core value at the heart of winning clients' trust is transparency across the business value chain and service propositions. For buyers of financial products and services this book aim's are to simplify the main issues addressed by the FSA regulatory directives and indeed provide ways of healthy engagement and communication with the industry and create confidence in the process for purchasing financial services, including questions to ask and references to use to aid better financial capability.

Which? Magazine's 'Money Maze' publication places some key and concerning questions that need to be addressed when it comes to the consumers' financial needs. From research, they argue consumers feel ostracised by the industry's opaque nature, that they do not have a voice in the development of the products and services they are offered and that the odds are stacked against them when it comes to forms of redress. Consumers also feel short changed by the industry in products and services value for money and as Which? point out; the regulators and other agencies need to help the consumer engage more effectively and productively with the industry. Yet as my investigation and interviews conducted for this book show, the RDR is giving the consumer a once in a lifetime opportunity to find their voice with the bias on remuneration in particular, placed back with the client.

At times I draw upon social science and include examples of psychological research that applies specifically to behavioural economics. This is because both public and private sector policy is now heavily tempered by understanding the psychology of those affected by its implementation. Where financial services are concerned, the focus is on financial capability and the effect individual judgmental biases have on financial decisions. Behavioural economics and social science themselves have their critics in those who may view human reactions as rational and with no place for irrational judgements and many benchmark experiments usually involve control groups in controlled environments. Yet without such 'social benchmarks' there is little to validate why markets crash, why two people with similar circumstances and wealth end up with very different outcomes. Support for the theories I address is shown in work completed by David de Meza and his colleagues at the London School of Economics, Otto Thorenson in his work on generic advice and the FSA themselves who released their baseline paper on UK financial capability which in turn gives credence to the need for an accepted focus on human nature's somewhat unpredictable relationship with finance.

The very title of this book is also worth attention. When I began research into the concept of trust between financial services organisations and their clients, it seemed that it was accepted that trust is a valuable and desired relationship. Yet as I researched further I found that trust is a hot topic that needs debate and further definition.

At a recent industry event hosted by the Social Market Foundation, 'trust in financial services' the Money Savings Experts Martin Lewis condemned the need for trust as dangerous. Yes, but it's not that simple.

Trust has several connotations being principally based on relationships between people where one party shows a willingness to rely on the actions of another. There should also be reasonable expectation (confidence) that those trusted will behave in a way beneficial to those doing the trusting.

Where it can all go pear shaped is when those who are trusted abuse the relationship and rely on the fact that the trusting party has little or no control. The concept of client to business trust within the financial services industry is therefore seen as a commodity and one that has suffered abuse. This has led to mistrust and (sometimes) misplaced trust and thus we have the regulatory changes to attempt to protect the customers' agenda and ensure business is held to account at all times.

This is all fine, but trust between people and institutions throughout the ages can be demonstrated as a natural disposition that is needed to avoid inertia, i.e. we need to trust to avoid just sitting on the edge of confidence in what is known and what is possible. We need to trust in our society to make things happen and live with a sense of optimism.

As we will see in chapter 5, where consumers' financial capabilities are investigated, the financial services industry must begin to understand they cannot get away with reliance on client inertia in applying teaser rates and features to products to entice customers in and expect trust to exist. Consumers are getting wise to such practices. Many now know that a nil percent credit card is effectively a Venus fly trap in it's 'reliance' on consumers forgetting to pay off the balance or missing a payment leading to a full APR to be charged.

So trust for me is an essential component of any relationship that demands respect and within financial services applies at two levels, transactional and emotional. It is in the final chapter 'The Trust Factor' where I account for strategies that can be employed by the organisation that will lead to a healthy exchange of trust and sustainable, profitable relationships for both parties.

Levels of trust for financial advice formed a large section of the evidence submitted by the FSA to the Treasury Select Committee (TSC) investigation into the effects of RDR. As we can see from table 1, the problem stems from 70% of adults not seeking financial advice and of the 30% who do, 39% do not trust the advice received. There is therefore much to do to ensure trust levels reach more appropriate levels.

Table 1. Levels of trust of financial advice.

	% of adults	% trusting financial advice	% not trusting financial advice
All		45.0	48.0
Using any adviser	30.6	60.0	39.0
Not using a financial adviser	69.4		

SOURCE: *Financial Services Authority, Ev 34*

Yet, Table 2 shows that those who seek advice from IFAs are more trusting of financial advice than those who use a bank adviser or an accountant or solicitor:

Table 2: Trust of financial advice by type of adviser

Received Professional advice from:	% of all adults	% trusting financial advice
IFA	18%	63%
Bank or Building society adviser	11%	55%
Accountant or solicitor	3%	53%

SOURCE: *Financial Services Authority, Ev 35*

And finally Table 3 shows the distribution of those who do and do not trust financial advice by age, with those between 30 and 49 showing the most mistrust of financial advice.

Table 3: Trust of financial advice by age

Age Band	Trust financial advice (45% of all adults)	Don't trust financial advice (48% of all adults)
Under 30 years old	25%	14%
30 — 49 years old	39%	36%
50 — 64 years old	20%	27%

SOURCE: *Financial Services Authority, Ev 35*

By no means is this book written as a panacea for the RDR journey and the confusion consumers seem to continue to face when engaging the retail investment markets. It does (I hope) act as a tool for best practice and as a reference companion for market participants and consumers alike for their journey to the new world of the RDR processes, or as a learning and development tool that may help with business' transitory issues and problems that may arise not just with the RDR but with any change management challenge that faces your industry.

With only 15 months to go to the RDR compliance deadline (if indeed it's not extended as the TSC recommend to 2014) all market participants, from the regulator to banks, IFAs, wealth managers and clients, have a final opportunity to collaborate constructively and co-build relationships that are reciprocal and mutually beneficial for all.

Chapter 1
The Key RDR Challenges

"Accept challenges, so that you may feel the exhilaration of victory".
George S Patton.

If we stand back, take a deep breath and view the challenges the UK financial industry faces over the coming 12 months or so to 1 January 2013 - RDR 'D Day' - we are initially overwhelmed by its implications and ramifications. The RDR is essentially the biggest change this industry has seen for more than two centuries. It's that huge. With such a challenge comes the need to map out the key steps to ensure change is managed and met head on, whilst also embracing the consumer's need for transparency and value in all business operations.

Before we start, Deloitte's research arm recently surveyed participants in the RDR market and the results showed an industry that is not yet ready for the challenge:

"Approximately a third (27%) of the 63 company delegates surveyed at Deloitte's recent event in London on RDR readiness, said they were still developing a strategic response, while 13% were focusing on engaging senior management on the topic. Only 11% said they were executing plans for implementation. The majority of these were life insurers. Company readiness for the FSA's Retail Distribution Review (RDR) is falling behind,"
SOURCE: *Deloitte, the business advisory firm March 2011.*

There is therefore still much to do.

1.1 The RDR implementation journey

With current investment advice practices closely allied with existing insurance and mortgage businesses, it is inevitable that the RDR has potentially far reaching implications for all involved in the financial services industry. It is clear that whilst the FSA's intentions may be good, the ramifications of such audacious regulatory change may prove difficult to predict, fathom and manage.

Past experience has taught us to be cautious when engaging regulatory reform and as Albert Einstein said: 'A true definition of madness is repeating the same action and expecting a different outcome.' We would therefore hope that the history of UK financial services regulation and its consequences have been properly studied by the regulator so that a positive outcome can be expected when the effects of the RDR are truly felt.

A key area that has clearly been ignored within the regulation of the industry is behavioural economics, which studies the effect of irrational behaviour on financial judgements and which also involves regulatory firms along with market participants. This is a subject we will explore in Chapter 5: how such regulatory imposition on such a dynamic industry is now tempered by behavioural studies and its affect on the consumer.

When launched in June 2006 the RDR wanted to fundamentally reconsider how investments were distributed to retail consumers in the UK. With the FSA now having published its consultation papers (with revisions to follow), we are now in the critical final implementation phase when it is crucial to understand the RDR's impact on businesses.

Through the RDR process, the FSA believes it has identified the various longstanding problems that impact on the overall quality of advice that restricts consumer confidence and trust in the UK investment market. In a world of principles-based regulation, satisfactory consumer "outcomes" are all important and the FSA is concerned with eliminating customer harm. Together with other elements of the FSA's retail strategy (e.g. Treating Clients Fairly [TCF], financial capability and Retail Mediated Activities Returns [RMAR]) the proposals are designed to tackle the major shortcomings identified within the existing regulatory framework.

Yet the very objectives of the RDR were confused when Hector Sants explained them to the Treasury Select Committee (TSC) in November 2010, simplifying the objectives from six:

- An industry that engages with consumers in a way that delivers more clarity for them on products and services
- A market which allows more consumers to have their needs and wants addressed
- Standards of professionalism that allow competitive forces to work in favour of consumers
- Remuneration arrangements that allow competitive forces to work in favour of consumers
- An industry where firms are sufficiently viable to deliver on their longer term commitments and where they treat their customers fairly
- A regulatory framework that can support delivery of all of these aspirations and which does not inhibit future innovation where this benefits consumers

To three:
- A transparent and fairer charging system
- A better qualification framework for advisers
- Greater clarity around the type of advice being offered
  🐦 #RDRBOOK

The important point to note is the objective surrounding the focus on consumers' 'needs and wants' has disappeared. A clear declaration that the original six remain is needed. Seemingly moving the goalposts at this late stage cannot help the considerable unease and discomfort felt by the industry with the deadline to RDR enforced compliance looming ever nearer. With the FSA calling on all investment adviser firms and product providers to consider how they will adapt to these challenging reforms, I outlay the key areas of contention. Firstly by pointing to the problems and then providing action points with solutions. If they are implemented as proposed, the RDR demands for transformation, modernised practices, significantly raised standards and the fair treatment of customers may be met and managed.

So what are the RDR challenges for the industry? Well it is very apparent that with any wide sweeping regulatory reform or government policy for that matter (think Conservative Prime Minister David Cameron's BIG SOCIETY agenda), confusion, mystification and unforeseen consequences may abound and only seek to confuse those who are affected. It is therefore important to outline the challenges to enable strategies to be devised. I have defined them into two camps - foreseen and unforeseen consequences.

AC charging

▨ **Charged when clear service agreed up-front with the client.**

▨ **Charged when commission is outlawed.**

▨ **Product neutral (no bias).**

▨ **Generated from cash a/c unit cancellation.**

▨ **Ongoing service.**

▨ **Applies to all Retail Investment Products (RIPs).**

▨ **Trail fees apply to business pre-2013 BUT technically banned January 2013**

1.2 Foreseen Consequences:
As mentioned the RDR intentions are laudable; to create a level playing ground for charging and bias firmly placed onto the consumer, away from the industry. So with the implementation stage well and truly underway we now see retail organisations facing the following challenges:

1. Adviser Charging - (AC)
Intermediaries:

Products and advisers will no longer be able to charge commission directly to their clients but have to re-structure their remuneration to a fee-based model. It is important to point out with these 'trail fees' banned after January 2013, a true 'solicitor style' fee structure needs to be employed where advisers charge for their time when advice is given.

Could RDR lead to higher charging?

There is certainly a risk of higher charging in the immediate aftermath of the 'scramble' to RDR compliance. Yet in the longer term such higher margins may be reduced.

Increased transparency on wholesale prices e.g. Factory Gate Pricing (FGP) where the adviser is paid up front or from the investor's policy, could increase competition as it enables end-customer behaviour, such as shopping around, which counteracts any upward pressure on AC. Price is an important driver for competition and the effect of the higher net worth (HNW) clients placing pressure on higher ACs will also see prices come down.

Could RDR lead to price discrimination?

In my view quite the opposite, there is an existing climate and culture of price discrimination through commission rebating so the RDR's transparency will aid behavioural change management to a fairer unbiased fee-charging structure. We are already seeing developments where providers are prepared to negotiate price to be charged to the client rather than commission to the adviser. Aviva's introduction of price and risk consultants is a good example of this.

2. Product Charging

It might be fair to say that the majority of product providers are behind the curve when it comes to 'RDR friendly' products and services. There is still plenty to do for product design, but it does give the industry a great opportunity to build ingenuity and high efficiency into its offerings.

Key areas for product ingenuity are around the style of charging structure adopted. As we shall see later when we investigate the industry value chain in Chapter 4, product charging is essential to get right in order to provide fair procurement of fees to the consumer.

Could RDR lead to inferior product quality?

The RDR should improve product quality because providers will want to ensure their services and products offer the best value as consumers will have greater clarity in comparing different products forcing providers into direct competition. With clear competition there is suddenly an incentive to improve products that benefit the consumer to get an edge on rivals. This strong competition is also expected to offer good service in terms of responsiveness and efficient handling of client support and requests. This will be a direct result of hourly fee billing where consumers will want quick response times to reduce their costs. Clarity on unbundling of fees associated with platforms and 'wraps' will also aid development of quality products within retail financial services.

Could RDR affect product suitability?

The trade-off between suitability of product and commission payments is removed by the RDR. This means that product providers and retail firms need to take into account their own charging structure before recommendations are made to the consumer. This inevitably leads to a trade off between suitability and time employed to arrive at a solution. In theory there should be more business turned down because the time needed to 'do it right' impacts on suitability. The additional time imposed by poor servicing has traditionally been paid for by cross-subsidy but who pays now the client?

3. Professionalisation

Advice is and will be driven by transparency and ethics. Advisers now have to pass the challenging (QCF) Level 4 diploma examinations, which have become effectively a license to trade. The independent advisory industry has already made admirable strides to ensuring those who want to stay in the new world order are reaching for this qualification.

'Specialist' adviser roles already exist in pension transfers, long-term care and equity release. However, these are tied to product advice in regulatory policing. The future may well see the need for specialist departments in adviser businesses with increased professionalism in their respective areas of expertise such as long term care advisers rather than product salesman. This increased 'professionalism' may mean an increase in the overall price of advice.

Independent or Restricted advice?

The general view is that currently and more importantly in 2013 onwards, independent advice is the "Gold Standard" for firms and its maintenance post-RDR compliance is highly desirable.

However, in reality most firms will find their independent status is compromised by a process-driven service offered through various distribution channels post-RDR. The internet, telephone, and face-to-face channels will all be utilised to a greater extent, yet it is probable that consumers will tend to want restricted

Implications of Restricted vs. Independent Advice...

- **Impact of outsourcing expertise to professionals.**

- **JP Morgan's survey of wealth managers uneven playing field created between 'generalists' and 'specialists' (e.g. GPs).**

- **Both areas of practice have the same qualification standard.**

- **Relevant Markets and Retail Investment Products (RIPs) need clear definition.**

- **Is it commercially sound to be either?**

- **Clarification on definitions and significance is imperative.**

advice as they will feel independent advice is for the higher net worth (HNW) clients only. This means a high quality of oral disclosure and potential polarisation of the industry (see unforeseen consequences) is therefore a reality with the mass market going direct for advice or intermediation and HNW retaining a niche independent advice market.

The Association of British Insurers (ABI) have conducted a considerable amount of research on business models and presented simplified advice as a possible solution where clients will start with an automated system of assessment of needs that will then move to a filtering of clients to the offer of restricted or full-blown independent advice. 🐦#RDRBOOK

Client needs?
A 'transformational' consumer relationship needs to be developed where flexibility and a customer first focus is key. Transactional relations may well fade, but will still play a role, particularly where simplified advice or execution only is employed.

4. Clarity of Products and Services
It is true to say that asymmetric (in-balanced or biased) information distorts competition in the market for financial products, making it difficult for consumers to choose an appropriate product. There is a lack of transparency about product charges, with rebating and discounting of stated charges being commonplace. Once products have been purchased, the service levels are reflected in limited evidence of switching if performance is not satisfactory.

There is unambiguous evidence of increasing demand for holistic long-term services and a clear consistent client proposition, which makes their development essential for RDR survival.

Platforms, Wraps and Nominee Services: bundling or unbundling?

🐦 #RDRBOOK

Platforms are the way clients and intermediaries access Retail Investment Products (RIPs). With the FSA's recently published paper CP10/29 which embellishes on CP10/2, this area has been highlighted as opaque by industry and consumers alike and is why so much attention is being given to the transparency of platform charges by the FSA post-RDR.

The regulator intends to make a compromise on the bundling/ unbundling of charges on wrap, platform and nominee services by allowing unbundling to continue but banning any cash rebate. This may mean higher administration charges and a compromise on transparency.

The 'Axa Elevate' wrap is a good example - due to some contractual ties with fund management groups they cannot unbundle all charges, which in Axa's opinion will only affect three percent of existing retail customers. Skandia concur in offering both unbundled and bundled charging structures. This may or may not help intermediaries meet RDR requirements.

> ## Platform Charging
>
> **Bundling:**
> ▥ **Platform and fund managers agree a management fee discount.**
>
> **Unbundling:**
> ▥ **Intermediary is free to choose funds.**

Intermediaries will be required to select platforms that are no more expensive than any other and confirm this is still the case annually. I believe the FSA's platform directives leave the following questions unanswered:

1. Will this lead to price competition between platforms or will they tend to settle to a norm?
2. How will financial advisers check annually that the platform they use for a particular client is offering best value?
3. Will fund rebates paid through extra units mean fund bias?

FSA's platform consultation paper:

▪ **Platform cash rebates to be banned, with rebates made instead in the form of units.**

▪ **Fund manager rebates to platforms allowed.**

▪ **Platforms to conduct 'timely' in specie re-registration.**

▪ **Advisers can use one platform and remain independent provided it is in clients' best interests.**

▪ **Regulator has ruled against forcing platforms to host specialist investments like tax elected funds.**

▪ **Providers will not face increased capital adequacy requirements.**

4. There is a requirement for a summary table on charges on client statements, showing for instance the fund cost (AMC or TER), the effective percentage rebate and the platform admin fees. Will this mechanism prevent additional share classes?

5. The FSA's insistence that best execution continues to apply essentially means that the investment process needs to alter to consider which platform could deliver the lowest set of charges for the recommended investments. The big sigh of relief that many let out in the Platform Papers stance regarding using single platforms will be short-lived.

As there is to be a differentiation between platforms and services which are auxiliary to investment management (to which the new rules will generally not apply) this surely creates blurred boundaries: i.e.

1. As fund managers can now pay platforms for admin, will this count against low cost products (such as Exchange Traded Funds (ETFs) and equities) that do not pay admin fees?

2. Customers will be able to stop payment to adviser firms. A client could then sack the IFA and retain the adviser charges in their account. Could platforms then accept direct clients?

3. Will the investors only pay for the service they require? For example, an investor might pay 1.5 percent for a fund, the fund charges 0.75 percent with a platform charging 0.25 percent for admin and adviser fees of 0.5 percent. An investor could go directly to the fund manager and pay only 0.75 percent. Alternatively will an adviser and lower up-front product fee be charged which will add to service transparency and client trust?

These questions represent some of the concerns and knowledge gaps created by RDR related regulatory consultation papers that need to be considered by the market practitioner in order to define the challenges and provide clear solutions.

5. Market Evolution

The market is incorporating new technological advancements and structures at a fast pace. The above platforms and wrappers are examples of technological developments that have taken place in recent years. They have given advisers the opportunity to offer consumers a more holistic service, involving more efficient portfolio management services. In addition, platforms aimed directly at consumers provide easy access to a wide range of products and enable individual portfolio management. However, aside from the potential benefits of platforms, the FSA has identified concerns around their charging structures, in particular relating to their complexity and lack of transparency.

Technology companies such as Prestwood, Capita Financial Software and Voyant continue to provide on-line cash-flow management and general financial management tools. As we shall see in later chapters, the next consumer generations (Y & Z) will be so important to target for financial companies if they want to maintain their competitive edge. This means social media and interactive online tools will need to be developed, giving consumers the ability to access advice easily and the industry the opportunity to educate on sound financial planning.

6. Business Model

Historically, RIPs in the UK were characterised at the provider level by large numbers of providers and advisers, with a number of different types of distribution channels. From the consumers' perspective the structure was one of independent advice given or execution only advice offered by various firms, paid for indirectly through commission.

This is starting to change with vertical integration (network creations, acquisitions, takeovers or mergers) now very apparent with some providers, particularly life assurance companies, acquiring interests in adviser firms.

A significant proportion of product business competition is aimed at persuading advisers to recommend a particular provider's products, rather than marketing the efficacy of products to consumers directly. Business models are structured around direct competition on the basis of factors such as past performance, reputation and price. At the distribution level, there is a perception that competition between advisers may be limited, as most consumers do not appear to shop around for advice. Any competition that does exist appears to be based on quality of service and access to products, rather than price. Commission bias has been identified as a feature of the market.

1.3 Unforeseen Consequences:

This is where the 'regulator bashers' have a field day and indeed there are many theories that the RDR is actually aimed at the fact that the retail financial services industry has long gone 'under the radar' where tax is concerned with commission remuneration's ability to avoid taxes. It is indeed the area of taxation that we begin to see some unintended repercussions:

1. Value Added Tax (VAT) and advice costs

Joint guidance issued in August 2010 by HMRC and the ABI attempted to clarify the VAT liability of advisers' remuneration. Advice only is taxable, they confirmed, while arranging the purchase of a financial product is exempt. Where clients receive both services, the "predominant" one determines the VAT liability.

However, possible confusion over which service outweighs the other has swayed some businesses toward the 'safety net' of separating their charges for the benefit of the taxman. This could provide a pragmatic solution that may avoid any retrospective VAT decision by HMRC, but by splitting the cost, this may actually incur VAT on part of the bill and thus this will inevitably be passed on to the consumer, giving higher fees.

The self-inflicted problems HMRC incurred in 2010 through its new income tax collection system, either taxing individuals too much or too little, may come to haunt the RDR where VAT charging is concerned. Neither advisers nor clients would welcome a notice stipulating VAT should have been charged when it was not and vice-versa.

VAT charging may become RDR's Achilles' heel.

Can the industry find an adequate solution to this issue?

Engage Partnership Ltd

Although good work is being produced thus far by interested parties such as the ABI, the Tax Incentivised Savings Association (TISA) and HMRC in the form of guidance notes on the VAT issue, it seems clear that VAT is to be charged on client receipt of advice only, not on purchase of a product (pension, investment, life or mortgage). Indeed HMRC's 2011 budget letter for the financial services sector highlights the need for clarity surrounding VAT charging as a key area to aid RDR transition. In this same light the danger of such uncertainty was highlighted by pension administrator Freedom SIPP's VAT dispute on charging which almost led HMRC to liquidate the SIPP giving the investors a potential £66 million tax charge headache if the scheme was de-registered. TISA is encouraging further work to be conducted on the VAT issue in particular to the clarification on the potential splitting of services and which service predominates where VAT is concerned for all market participants including advisers, product providers and fund managers. Clear guidance will strongly aid the purpose of consistent value chain transparency.

🐦 #RDRBOOK

Fees and charges

KPMG's July 2010 YouGov survey of more than 3,000 consumers found that less than a third would be prepared to pay for one hour's professional financial advice. Of those that would pay, more than a half would only be prepared to pay £50 or less while only one percent would be willing to pay over £200. The economics of the RDR will therefore be hard for the financial industry to balance.

> ### Consumers - a challenge?
>
> **KPMG's YouGov survey:**
>
> ▓ **Consumers unwilling to pay for financial advice.**
>
> ▓ **£50 ceiling for majority of those that will pay.**
>
> ▓ **IFAs are the most trusted source of financial advice.**
>
> ▓ **Providers will struggle with RDR transition.**

ABI research also paints a bleak picture with 50 percent of consumers stipulating they will not pay for advice.

In time, consumers will realise the true value in paying for advice - but only when fees and the value chain are transparent and clearly communicated.

ABI research also calculated that on average advice took seven hours, 40 minutes at a cost of £670 to the firm to deliver. Therefore, the level of charges and fees needs to be carefully considered from the consumer's point of view to ensure a profitable margin is met and fees are affordable. This then can determine the restricted or independent and simplified advice route. Intermediaries need to be bold and not under-sell themselves. What sits behind the move to fee charging is the move to 'professionalism' and transparency that pervades the FSA's RDR mantra.

In this case a demanding juxtaposition is placed on RDR compliance in the increase of industry professional standards and fair and transparent charging. As we have seen, front line sales advisers will have to promote their professionalism and ethics at all levels as never before and ensure they are competent and fair in their charging of fees, along with ensuring they remain competitive. How will this potential conflict of interest play out?

Which? 🐦**#RDRBOOK**
Consumers do not understand the market:

- **Lack of trust.**
- **Restricted advice is misleading.**
- **Concern on cost of advice.**
- **Independence is preferred.**
- **Transparency needed.**

Consumer perspective

The current structure from the consumer's perspective is one of independent advice given or execution only service (non-advice) offered by various means, which are paid for indirectly through commission.

As a commission culture still permeates, consumers see advice as free so a move to fee-based charging may actually cause consternation in the short-term. ABI research found worrying 50 percent of consumers will not pay for advice and as the consumers currently see no initial expense through the commission system, that financial advice is worthless! (Figure 1.1).

A contraction of IFAs and advisers in general is expected and quoted by some by as much as 20-50 percent. This leaves the consumer with a potential gap in the advice market and a significant loss of experience for the industry.

Figure 1.1: How much do consumers think financial advice is worth?

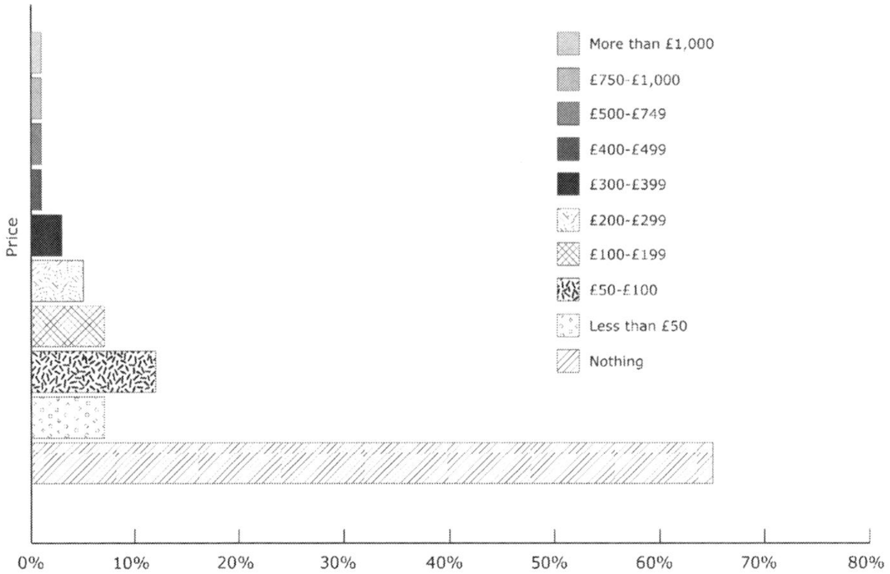

SOURCE: *ABI Quarterly Consumer Survey, 2010 Q4. 2608 Consumers.*

Front line adviser skills

There are two areas here that require urgent attention;

1. The issue surrounding exempting (or grandfathering) those with years of experience from the professionalisation that the RDR demands.

2. The soft skills or emotional intelligence that is now required for those advisers and staff involved with consumer engagement

Grandfathering: This is a cross industry term that says those workers with plenty of relevant experience should be allowed certain exemptions or allowances that acknowledge their relevant 'on the job' knowledge. With the high RDR accountability measures and its attempt to create a level playing field on charges and fees, we are seeing those with great experience and knowledge still have to undertake examinations to QCF level 4 standard and beyond. The question that follows is will there be an industry brain drain as experienced advisers decide they do not want to take the exams and will either sell out or retire?

Soft Skills: While the emphasis given by the regulator is predominantly on examination achievement i.e. technical skills, the day-to-day fee based client consultation process now demands a complete understanding of the value of the adviser's services. This and the underlying psychological contract clients have with their finances is their value chain. Alongside the shift of consumer perception of 'free' advice under the commission structure, this means we now see a need to address people skills. These will be needed to ensure the engagement and maintenance of clients' interest and trust post January 2013.

Having the right people in the right place with the right skill set is quite profound and not addressed at all by the professionalism demanded, something we'll expand upon through focusing on the value chain and behavioural economics (Chapters 4 and 5).

So whether foreseen or unforeseen, the consequences and subsequent challenges for the UK retail financial services are great and firstly need to be tackled by a fundamental understanding of the value chain.

1.4 Summary

The RDR challenges are immense and not to be underestimated. Organisations are now attempting to position themselves to gain the best possible momentum running into the final year through to RDR 'D-Day'. If market participants can recognise, communicate and manage the challenges with well-structured change management strategies then there will be an opportunity to dominate the market space come 2013.

To meet those challenges:
- A firm and consistent change management programme needs to be employed across the business to understand, plan and implement a coherent RDR implementation strategy.
- Ignore the unintended consequences at your peril; recognising

and tackling the RDR elephants in the boardroom is a must.

- Engagement and education for the consumer needs to happen quickly in order for an understanding and acceptance of the value of fee based charging.

Chapter 2

Evolution of Financial Services Regulation and Business

"It is not the strongest of the species that survive, nor the most intelligent, but the one most responsive to change"
Charles Darwin.

As we move through the challenges to understand the value chain and psychological issues surrounding retail finance advice, it is important to understand how we have got to this position with the RDR.

In other words why have the UK regulators decided to introduce this system as a mandatory 'fait accompli' and where indeed does the financial organisation fit whether it be product provider or retail advice based company?

2.1 A history of regulation

Figure 2.1 is a timeline mapping out the events that have taken the industry to this stage of compulsory qualification and business model change. As you may see, it makes interesting and very relevant reading when we contemplate the effect the RDR will have on both the industry and consumer.

Figure 2.1: The Journey to RDR

UK FINANCIAL SERVICES REGULATION RDR TIMELINE:

1981: A 'disorderly' financial services market prompts the Thatcher Government to appoint Professor L C B Gower to conduct a commission examining investor protection.

1984: Gower recommends a business regulatory regime to curb excesses and a maximum commission agreement to stop prices rising. Gower expects the government to reject the maximum commission idea. Self Regulatory Organisations (SROs) were seen as the best way forward by the government, yet one SRO introduced a threshold to commission hard disclosure rulings. This was abolished by the Director of Fair Trading on the grounds of artificially holding prices up. This meant rising commission levels!

1985: Securities and Investments Board Ltd (SIB) incorporated to enforce a new framework for investor protection. It was proposed that alongside the SIB would be a Marketing of Investments Board (MIB) to cover the regulation of pre-packaged investments.

1986: The Financial Services Act put into place comprehensive regulation covering persons performing investment business giving specific advice. This was to stop individuals purporting to give independent advice when actually tied or appointed representatives of single or a small number of firms. This became known as polarisation.

1988: Basel I, the Basel Accord. International central bankers set minimum capital requirements for banks.

1995: The collapse of Barings Bank and other notable financial scandals meant an end to self-regulation of the financial services industry. SIB revoked the recognition of Financial Intermediaries, Managers and Brokers Regulatory Association (FIMBRA) as an SRO and members moved to the Personal Investment Authority (PIA).

1997: SIB changes its name to Financial Services Authority

1999: Office of Fair Trading (OFT) investigates polarisation of the industry due to PIA rules and finds them anti-competitive, thus FSA removes them.

2002: FSA Consultancy Paper 121 (CP121) advocates reforming of polarisation rules and adviser charging, yet this is not well received by the industry.

2004: EU Markets in Financial Instruments Directive (MiFID) introduced to supersede Investment Services Directive (ISD), to allow passporting rights of financial services across the EU with the emphasis on home state supervision known as 'maximum harmonisation'.

Basel II introduced using a 3-pillar concept to ensure capital allocation, operational/credit risk and reduce regulatory arbitrage.

2005: UK Polarisation abolished.

2006: RDR announced by FSA as in its view the distribution model was broken and bias needed to be given to the consumer.

2007: Financial economic crisis hits all major financial service organisations and creates a climate of fear and distrust for consumers.

2009: Basel III introduced to bolster previous accords, bank capital adequacy and liquidity, which is closely followed by the 'Basel for the insurers': Solvency II, a three pillar strategy focusing on transparency, governance, risk and capital requirements.

EU consultation by commission on legislative steps for the Packaged Retail Investment Products (PRIPs) Initiative, a directive to bring transparency and sales rules to the PRIPs market to protect standards and rebuild trust following the financial crises.

2010: UK General election ousts the Labour government with the electorate undecided on who to govern following the financial crises and politicians' expenses scandals. The coalition government decides to go along with Conservative proposals to replace the FSA with the Consumer Protection and Markets Authority (CPMA) and in its June consultation paper the treasury confirms the CPMA will uphold the RDR, alongside a more pro-active and interventionist approach to financial regulation.

2010 November sees the House of Commons (HOC) debate the RDR with significant emphasis on professionalism and grandfathering of existing experience/qualifications. Hector Sants clarifies the issues surrounding the change of RDR directives by reducing them from six to three.

2011/2012 onwards: (As I see it)...

- Clarification is expected on the FSA consultancy papers, particularly on platforms and adviser charging (AC). The HMRC is even challenging the definition of AC.
- Treasury Select Committee to follow the HOC RDR debate with a recommendation on RDR implementation cause and effect incorporating the treasury paper on simple financial products and work completed on behavioural economics/financial capability analysis.
- Establishment of a macro-prudential regulator, the Financial Policy Committee (FPC) within the Bank of England to monitor and respond to systemic risks.
- The FSA replaced and split in two by a Prudential Regulatory Authority (PRA) headed by Hector Sants and a Financial Conduct Authority (FCA) (Accountants will enjoy the 'affiliate' acronym) headed by former Chief Executive of Hong Kong's Securities and Futures Commission (SFC) Martin Wheatley. FSA to oversee 27,000 firms and share 2000 with PRA (See Fig 2.2)
- Expect a tougher approach to regulation of banks in particular after the much-maligned FSA report on Royal Bank of Scotland collapse which Bill Knight and Sir David Walker are currently reviewing at the request of the Treasury Select Committee.
- Industry (IFA's) will continue pressuring the regulator on grandfathering momentum
- The platform and wrap market to become ever more competitive with some big names in the Life sector going through mergers or acquisitions.
- Simplified advice to either gain traction or be abandoned altogether.

SOURCE: *Engage Partnership Limited RDR discussion paper.*

It is important to note that the above timeline does not encompass any self-regulatory measures taken by industry. For example since the credit crunch banks have been operating with more capital and liquidity in line with Basel III. There have also been substantial moves towards recovery and resolution plans, known as 'living-wills' so that financial institutions never again have to turn to the taxpayer for support.

Figure 2.2: Roles and accountabilities in new financial regulatory system.

Parliament
Parliament sets the legislative framework and holds the Government to account (for the regulatory framework) and holds the regulatory bodies to account (for performance of their functions)

The Chancellor of the Exchequer and the Treasury
The Chancellor is responsible for the regulatory framework and for all decisions involving public funds

UK regulatory system

Bank of England
Protecting and enhancing the stability of the financial system of the United Kingdom

FPC
Identifying and monitoring systematic risks and taking action to remove or reduce them (including through directions and recommendations to the PRA and FCA)

subsidiary

PRA
Prudentially regulating banks, insurers and complex investment firms

FCA
Protecting and enhancing confidence in financial services and markets, including by protecting consumers and promoting competition

SOURCE: *HM Treasury A new approach to financial regulation; Blueprint for reform*

2.2 Current issues

Whichever way we wish to interpret the timeline of events above (and other related issues), we cannot get away from the fact that the despite changes in government regulatory outlook and political persuasion, we reach the conclusion that market dynamics are virtually impossible to predict and regulate.

Angela Knight, Chief Executive of the British Bankers' Association, interestingly points the finger at governmental management of public finances in apportioning blame for the recent financial turmoil. Her view is that those countries who managed their public spending well before the 2008 banking crises are recovering well, not those who allowed their public spending to "balloon". When it comes to regulatory reform Angela Knight argues this should be part of the picture along with healthy debates between business and society.

On the issue of regulatory reform, Ms Knight may have a point. At the time of writing we are again seeing a coalition government placing its own personality on regulation of financial services. It is breaking up former Prime Minister Gordon Brown's 'baby' the FSA and bringing in the Prudential Regulatory Authority (PRA) and the Financial Conduct Authority (FCA). If we look at our timeline this has a similarity with the introduction of the SIB and MIB in the 1980s i.e. a two top-tier body (twin peaks) regulation of financial services (particularly as the Consumers Protection and Markets Authority (CPMA) has already been superseded).

Indeed Professor LCB Gower's examination of investor protection in 1981-85 recommended against the MIB and SIB due to confusion and costs that could occur. This with the issues surrounding the polarisation rules begs the question: does this look familiar in relation to the RDR?

What we seem to be experiencing is a regulatory 'memory loss' in connection with the RDR, despite its laudable aims of consumer bias and fairness. We are again witnessing a new set of regulatory bodies being formed around investor protection ideals. Yet again we are also seeing unintended consequences as per Chapter 1 that potentially will undermine the RDR and the success of retail financial advice.

Surely to succeed in the future we have to ensure that mistakes of the past are taken into account? If they are not, such dramatic enforced change would be dangerous to any industry. Maybe the regulators along with people in general suffer from 'hyperbolic discounting' i.e. favouring short term over long-term proposals. History has shown that the financial services market is virtually impossible to predict and therefore regulate. The market represents a mass pool of the human psyche, as we have seen, with consumers failing to demonstrate economic rationality, ignoring price signals, and being undiscerning in relation to purchase of financial services, can the RDR really provide an all encompassing fair regulatory solution?

I would argue yes; and to demonstrate that the industry needs to be addressed at various levels i.e. segmented. We may begin to see how such a demanding and potentially opaque regulatory backdrop can be engaged and the RDR succeed in its objectives.

2.3 Financial advice
Firstly, looking at how retail financial sales have progressed will help us understand what will be a successful architecture for any client facing business model.

What is financial planning?
There are many ways to best describe financial planning. But the following diagram is a common used example of the main stages that make up this process. The RDR rightly demands that the client is at the heart of each stage of this process, and follows a holistic theme of supporting lifestyle goals and objectives. This means a structure designed around a service without the need of a product.

Figure 2.3: 6 step financial planning process

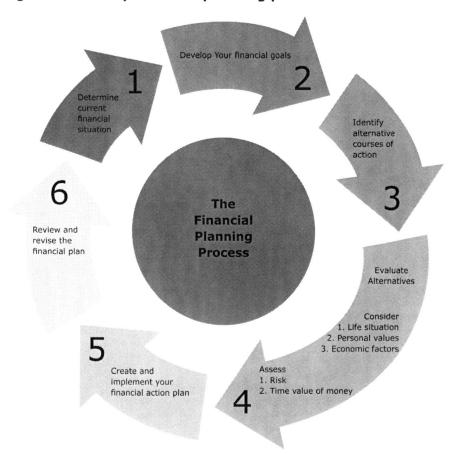

SOURCE: *Engage partnership ltd*

Such a service now demands a 'revisit' to the importance of 'soft skills'; the emotional intelligence needed to understand the client's psychological relationship with their finances. There is now no doubt that it will be a full job to nurture and maintain client trust by ensuring transparency of the value chain and fee disclosure is clearly communicated.

Yet how are we going to ensure clients comprehensively understand the value of engaging fee based financial service organisations particularly with the loss of faith and trust post credit crunch?

Figure 2.4 gives a timeline of the evolution of such soft skills, which makes an interesting overlay to the 2.1 regulatory time line

Figure 2.4: Evolution of financial advice

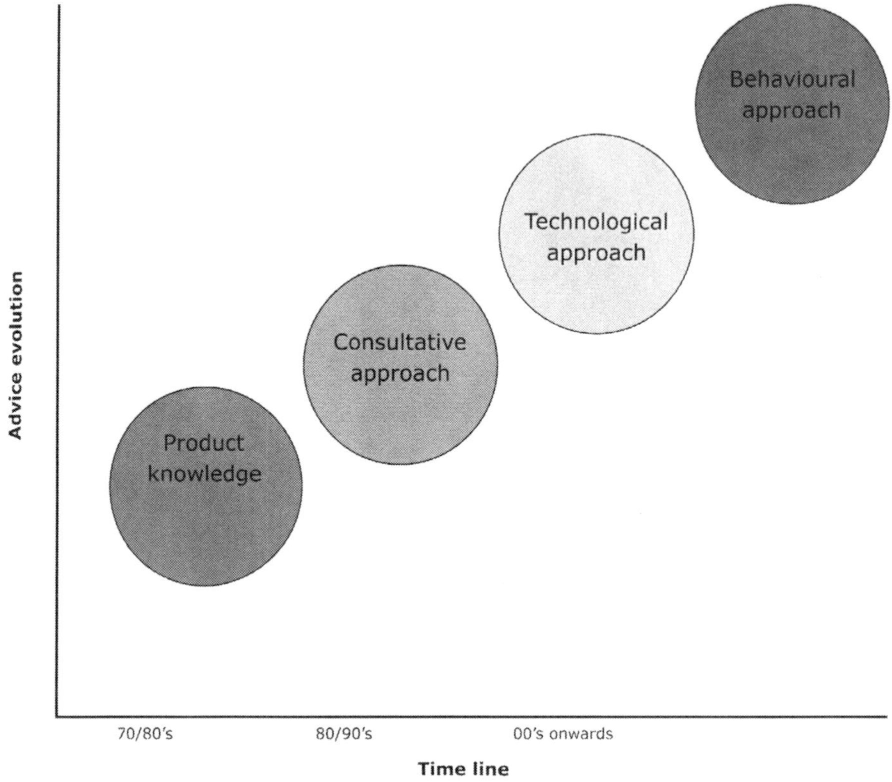

What this diagram is telling us is that maybe the pendulum had swung too far and we had a skewed view of technical excellence and competence (which is a move away from client-centric support) as the all-important skill set. Although these skills will remain important where front line client engagement is involved, we MUST now engage with clients from an understanding of psychological means i.e. behavioural finance.

The evolution of financial advice within the business-to-business (B2B) or business-to-customer (B2C) format was initially strongly influenced by authors of best sellers such as Miller and Heiman (Strategic selling) and Neil Rackham (Spin Selling). They can be described as transactionally based techniques: knowing price, product and market dynamics. Then individuals such as David Maister (Trusted Adviser), Ford Harding (Rainmaking), Daniel Goleman (Emotional Intelligence) and Keith Dugdale and David Lambert (Smarter Selling), introduced the importance of understanding of the personalities involved and behavioural dynamics, a transformational approach to sales and financial advising.

If the latter model is adopted (and there is evidence in the market at present) then client relations with financial planning and their aspirations for their future will be better understood, enhanced and encouraged for their and the industry's betterment.

"We found a big difference between what customers said was important and what actually drove their behaviour. **Customers insisted price and product aspects were the dominant factors** that influenced their opinion of a supplier's performance and, as a result, their purchasing decisions.

Yet when we examined what actually determined how customers rated a vendor's overall performance, **the most important factors were product or service features and the overall sales experience.**

The upside of getting these two elements right is significant: a primary supplier seen as having a **high-performing sales force can boost its share of a customer's business by an average of 8 to15 percentage points."**

McKinsey Quarterly, May 2010.

There is now plenty of evidence that conduct risks associated with financial advice are of most interest and importance to the regulators. The FSA has published one of two key papers on risk, conduct, with prudential risk yet to be announced.

We can see from this paper alone that the regulation surrounding risk can be focused on three areas:

1. Asymmetry (imbalance) of information available to consumers and providers: This means a discrepancy in the balance of information available giving little learning opportunity for market participants
2. Limited financial capability: A risk of information process overload
3. Systematic behavioural biases: As discussed in Chapter 5; procrastination, hyperbolic discounting (favouring short not long term), loss aversion, buyer's remorse and favouring the status quo bias.

This confirms that knowledge and practice of behavioural economics and finance are integral new competencies demanded by the regulators for financial services in the RDR world. Does this represent evidence that the Government and regulators are finally acknowledging the fact that financial services cannot be controlled by the traditional model based on the 'hard facts' of the market, but by incorporating the psychological aspects that have previously been ignored?

There is certainly compelling evidence when we look at statistics on sales impact;

Figure 2.5: Impact of salesman.

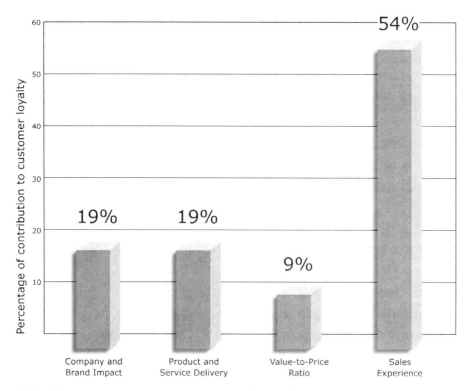

SOURCE: *Customer experience diagnostic 2010.*

As per the McKinsey findings, it's the sales experience that counts, not just pricing, branding or product delivery. David Lambert, Director of Training and Development consultancy IOWEU, stipulates it's all about 'relationship capital': high relationship capital is characterised by multiple, strong (Partner) relationships with people of power and influence'. This, along with the Government and regulator incentives, places the emphasis on the behavioural approach.

Financial planning tools
With the development and introduction of new technology within financial services we are seeing more areas of financial planning addressed than ever before. Gone are the days where a simple one-

page fact-find on a client's objectives was enough. There are now various tools, which we'll explore in greater detail in Chapter 10, that enable financial service organisations to understand far more clearly a client's relationship with money matters.

Cashflow modelling: Client's income and outgoings are mapped against their lifestyle goals. Trade-offs are arranged to ensure objectives are met.

Asset allocation: Tools that map out allocation exposure to certain asset classes.

Risk Profiling: Ensuring a client's attitude to investment risk is matched to their corresponding investment portfolio risk.

Net Asset Reporting: Online real time consolidated accounting of all a client's investable assets.

Platforms: One stop shop for providers to place their funds and products to be purchased by clients through financial advisers.

All such tools can impress and certainly cashflow modelling in particular allows clients to engage with their psychological relationship with money (fiscal psychological contract) and work out what trade-offs are needed to ensure lifestyle goals are met. Yet on their own they are still not enough for financial planning to succeed. Again it is the soft questions combined with understanding and matching the buyer's journey that is imperative.

2.4 Products

Part of the problem with retail financial services is the fact that both the consumer and the financial service professional are often overwhelmed by the choice of products available.

From the development of with profit funds in the 1950s through to synthetics (artificial simulation) hedge and exchange traded funds, we have seen an explosion in the product providers' offerings available. According to Forbes magazine, by June 2010 there were more than 9,000 mutual funds available for private investment.

This brings the 'Buridan's ass' problem - with so many opportunities, consumers tend not to act. The 'nudge' philosophy (see Chapter 5) of providing a few options where one of them is mandatory is a possible solution here, yet in a free democratic market, it is the individual who ostensibly has to make the choice to invest and then manage the portfolio or outsource to a professional.

As we will see in the next chapter from the value chain analysis, the RDR is attempting to address the total expense ratio (TER) problem of reduction in yield due to the effect of multiple layers of charging.

The emphasis is therefore moving to 'unbundling' charges i.e. ensuring all charges are clear and transparent for the consumer and easier to understand. This also brings to the fore the need for product providers to re-design products to become RDR friendly. This will mean lower charging, no rebates (subject to clarification) to third parties and clear boundaries around charges and fee payment facilities.

The HM Treasury's paper on Simple Product offers a realistic solution to issues already discussed such as making sense of choices, behavioural factors and low levels of shopping around that mean consumers suffer when choosing where to invest and which product is most suitable. Indeed previous incentives such as the Charges, Access, Terms (CAT) and Stakeholder Standards introduced in 1999 initially devised for ISAs and then residential mortgages products failed to produce the desired transparency and fairness in product design. This was simply because it became too difficult for product providers to offer price capped products when they were free to offer non-capped products. 🐦 #RDRBOOK

Simple product essentially entails a limited number of standardised features to aid consumer understanding and provide confidence in appropriate product choice. This, along with simplified advice, has seen a great flurry of focus of late. The FSA's paper on product intervention (DP 11/1), a much-awaited paper on simplified and restricted advice focuses on designing products that incorporate transparency in cost and design and the related regulatory issues surrounding the life cycle of the product. Figure 2.6 gives a good example of how the regulators see the value proposition of regulating products though their life cycle, with the RDR increasing focus on the earlier stages in this particular value chain.

Figure 2.6: Product life cycle

Problems	Exploitative pricing and design features, disregard of how products might behave, unfair contract terms	Exploitation of consumer behavioural traits (risk appetite, inertia)	Misalignment of Firm and consumer interests leading to: Unsuitable advice Mis-selling	Unclear responsibility post-sales Lack of information on product performance or review of appropriateness in changing scenarios Churning/lack of persistency Lack of continuing consumer care Further unsuitable sales to "correct problems"
	Development	Distribution stratergies	Point-of-sale	Post-sales handling

Financial promtions

Traditional focus of FSA intervention

Increased focus under the new stratergy

SOURCE: *FSA Product intervention DP 11/1.*

The Social Markets Foundation's (SMF) recent proposal of kite-marked products is interesting in ensuring a product is standardised and mandated as fair. This would involve extending the open market option and allowing investors to browse the money advice services website which would become the 'go to' place for investment product comparison. According to the SMF's John Springford, this would give unhampered consumer choice, encourage competitive pricing and ensure the mass market is catered for, not just the higher net worth investors.

This means if the regulator was to create kite marking for fair products then they would be setting transparent standards. In turn this would encourage fair and transparent competition and pricing in the market, not price capping or restriction of the market by direct intervention. Certainly where stakeholder pensions are concerned such product simplification did encourage healthy competition which resulted in a product price drop.

The end result is that product providers are beginning to realise that they need to dramatically change their design procedures and business models to ensure compliance with the new regulations and at a more basic level to simply survive.

FSA DP 11/1: Product Intervention

- Stipulates RU64, which requires advisers to justify recommendations of non-stakeholder pensions, maybe extended to other retail markets.
- This may mean price capping is not needed to encourage fair charging
- Not all market participants (life companies in particular) will be in favour of product intervention either directly or indirectly

2.5 Summary

As we shall see, Chapter 5 describes behavioural economics which spills over quite nicely into the arena of the retail industry development to date. In understanding how and why policy and regulation has been structured alongside its implementation with how the industry has reacted may provide a (very) rough guide to how the industry may cope and change post RDR implementation. In order to navigate future challenges:

- A comprehensive review of historical regulatory mistakes and biases needs to be reflected upon and employment of behavioural economic principles needs to be added to regulatory supervision.
- It's relationship capital that counts along with product, technical knowledge and relevant regulatory competencies. A focus on economic behavioural understanding, financial capability and

relational skills is now upon us and should be embraced by all market participants.

- Product providers, regulators and the consumer need to collaborate practically on clarity of information, transparency of charges and fairness of product choice in the market.

Chapter 3

Organisational Change and Transparency

"If we don't change our direction we're likely to end up where we're headed."
Chinese Proverb

The shift from a commission-based model to a fee-based model is by no means an easy task and will no doubt lead to behavioural change for firms. This in turn may lead to a focus on return on investment and profitability of the relationship with their clientele. This is down to the fact that the 'old style' cross subsidies that commission-based firms generated within the business (e.g. supporting unprofitable operations which might generate profits in the future) may now move to a focus on high value customer relations. In turn, they may well be less willing to accept large numbers of clients who are perceived as relatively low value.

'Militant' or conspiracy theories have abounded around those who are generally sceptical of change. The fact that the RDR is regulator driven gives such a view more potency, as the regulator's relations with financial services has been strained by the introduction of the RDR. The attrition of IFAs and associated brain-drain from the industry (quoted as much as 30 percent upwards), the RDR favouring the banks, polarisation of the market and exclusion of the mass market to independent financial advice are all strong and worrying accusations. As we will see later in Chapter 6 (business models), the market could move back to tied agents and appointed representatives who only give restricted advice. A simplified advice model could become the most popular distribution channel (if this is not abandoned) and there is no doubt that the industry will lose a number of its financial advisers, back office staff and there is already a certain amount of vertical integration going on as I write.

Yet we are seeing such change across other industries, for example the public sector in particular is suffering unprecedented cuts driven by the government's austerity measures, so why should financial services be any different? While it is probably unfair to levy a pointed finger at the regulators on a coercive front, the issue is rather that RDR directives could have been better planned and communicated in a more inclusive manner than they have been.

We are certainly witnessing the professionalisation of the industry with financial advisers having to meet higher qualification standards to continue to practice within the timeline given. We see issues surrounding grandfathering of qualifications being disallowed and IFAs in particular finding this difficult to understand when individuals with a wealth of experience are deemed technically inferior to new entrants to the industry who have a diploma in financial planning. Such enforced change may lead to a 'victim mentally' and thus may become detrimental to the change strategy itself. It is certainly why we are now witnessing the industry lobbying the government's treasury select committee, political figures such as the finance secretary Mark Hoban as well as FSA's and PBU's Hector Sants to better understand the effect of the RDR on the market.

Organisational Development

- to improve an organisation's visioning, empowerment, learning and problem solving processes,
- through an ongoing, collaborative management of organisational culture
- with special emphasis on the culture of intact work teams and other team configurations -
- using the consultant-facilitator role and the theory and technology of applied behavioral science, including action research.

French & Bell 1999

3.1 What is Organisational Change?

What we are witnessing is a drive for cultural and climate change across financial services and indeed one that forces us into unknown territory. As we have seen from the first chapter there are implicit and explicit issues, mystification and unintended consequences that may well cause huge problems for organisations once the RDR is in place. The issue is of course that we don't yet fully understand how the landscape will look in 2013 and beyond. So with such a quandary it may be helpful to look into key issues, areas and theory surrounding organisational change that by no means provide all the answers or questions but may act as a guide to RDR change and transparency in business.

There are various definitions of organisational development that will apply and be useful as we travel on the RDR change management journey. Warren Bennis (1969)[1] defined change as a complex educational strategy intended to change the beliefs, attitudes, values and structures of organisations so they may better adapt to new technologies, markets, challenges and the dizzying rate of change itself. Various other researchers define change in a similar way involving mainly top down long-term approaches that involve the whole of the organisation.

With such a broad definition comes the need to specify individual stages or attributes that change might bring to the company. With a focus on process and culture we can begin to foster a team spirit within the group that drives momentum and commitment to the change objectives. A focus on collaboration can mean the company has a far better chance of successfully implementing the change on a sustained basis with full participation and involvement across the business. Too many times business leaders inform staff on a 'need to know' basis regarding the change ahead which can only lead to fear and resistance at some stage down the line.

[1] Bennis Warren G. 1969. Organisational Development: Its Nature, Origins and Prospects. Addison-Welsey Publishing company.

We must remember that organisations are complex social systems, interconnected by all forms of modern day communication, so any negative views held may spread like wildfire hindering, or sometimes derailing, change. The idea or end objective should be to create a win-win scenario, where objectives and goals are shared, while engagement to successfully complete the change programme is total across all levels of the company.

Strategic change is important to get right across the organisation whether the change is enforced or not. It concerns the full scope of the organisation's activities, matching activities to resources and the market environment, along with having huge implications on decision-making and the long-term direction of the organisation. It therefore makes sense that any planning around RDR transition needs to be long term, strategic, encompasses a short and long term perspective and copes with the ever fiercer competitive forces of the market.

3.2 Change Management Strategies that Work

As the RDR presents its unique challenges, we begin to see how a well thought out change management process will provide big benefits to a business. There is again various research that we may draw upon to aid such a process. Kurt Lewin's (1947)[2] three-stage cycle model of unfreezing, freezing and unfreezing the change process is perhaps one of the most well known. This is essentially moving from comfort to discomfort through managed phases, which

**A three stage model of change
Lewin (1951)**

Unfreezing through;
- Disconfirmation
- Creation of guilt and anxiety
- Psychological safety

Moving through cognitive restructuring;
- Identify with new role model
- Environmental scanning

Refreezing;
- Total personality and self concept
- Significant relationships

[2] Burnes Bernard. 2004. Kurt Lewin and the planned approach to Change A Re-appraisal. *Journal of Managment Studies*. 41:6. 977-1002.

then leads to a desired new stage, or culture that is then frozen. So far with the RDR and regulator, there has definitely been plenty of discomfort with little guidance on how we get to the RDR 'comfort zone' if indeed one exits at all.

Organisational learning is another key process - essentially it is project management in deciding on the desired outcome and then working backwards to work out the steps or process needed to get there (Chris Argyris 1992)[3]. Such reflective work will help build in contingency plans as and when necessary as no change management process is smooth or generally sticks to Plan A. Adaptability may then be assessed and factored into the programme which will enable those responsible for the RDR change management programme to 'macro-manage' as and when necessary to encourage behavioural and structural development or re-alignment.

An interesting concept is Peter Senge's 'learning organisation' (1990)[4]. Here the process evolves around the organisation's capability to facilitate staff learning and continuously transforms itself. This is obviously built from a strong desire from the organisation to learn, a commitment to generating and transferring knowledge, an openness to the external environment and a shared vision incorporating systems thinking. Organisations that operate a 'flatter' structure are normally associated with such a strategy as they avoid the barriers to communication that the traditional hierarchical organisations attract. Yet with financial services companies, particularly in the banking sector, such hierarchical structures dominate, which may be one of the reasons why consumers feel excluded or confused by the industry's inconsistent use of information. This is something that has been severely criticised, particularly during the post financial crises period.

Institutional theory, which explains why organisations are what they

---

[3] Argyris Chris (1992) *On organizational learning.* Oxford: Blackwell.
[4] Senge, P. 1990. The Fifth Discipline: The Art and Practice of the Learning Organisation. *The Fifth Discipline, Random House Inc.* 484-491.

are (Paul DiMaggio & Walter Powell 1983)[5], is an area commonly forgotten when organisational behaviour is debated. The concept of RDR transition and compliance has been viewed as coercive (political), normative isomorphic (professionalisation), mimetic isomorphic strategy (modelling) or on the other hand as a new innovative entrepreneurial strategy in its own right. What I mean by this is that there are many views on the reasons for RDR and thus it's helpful to understand how they may play out when such wide reaching and industry changing change programmes are instigated.

Institutional theory also gives a positive slant on the change process the RDR brings. We are witnessing some new innovative business models being structured around the RDR principles that may actually provide the industry with an entrepreneurial approach. The use of technology and social media is beginning to be a must-have strategy which is aiding the consumer education process surrounding financial capability. I devote a whole chapter to this later on because with modern and state-of-the-art technology and communication channels, consumers may benefit from the 'isomorphic' activity that the RDR is now forming amongst market practitioners. This in fact feeds one of the original six RDR principles of educating consumers on their financial planning needs, in my opinion probably the most important.

There is certainly plenty of copying or 'mimetic' activity occurring, with copying of business models deemed successful elsewhere. Yet the issue is, are such models truly RDR compliant? Remember we just do not know the correct questions to ask until we actually arrive at our destination. There are those businesses who claim RDR compliance when they actually are not and those that are worrying about compliance when they already meet the rules. As we have seen challenges and issues surrounding the true nature and structure of adviser charging, product costs and the nature

[5] DiMaggio, P and Powell, W. 1983. The Iron Cage Revisited: Institutional Isomorphism and Collected Rationality in Organisational Fields. *American Sociological Review.* Vol 48, No 2, 147-160.

of bundling or unbundling have a long way to play out, so at present are we dealing with unknown unknowns? If so, great care needs to be taken in the change management process.

3.3 Change in Practice

So it's all well and good you may say, quoting organisational change theory and social science concepts that may be applicable and relevant to RDR organisational change management strategies, but what about the real world of the RDR change and mystery that surrounds the concept?

"Unknown Unknowns"

"There are known knowns; there are things we know we know. We also know there are known unknowns; that is to say we know there are some things we do not know. But there are also unknown unknowns – the ones we don't know we don't know".

Former US Secretary of State Donald Rumsfeld.
February 2002.

Well the first point to make is that again we are really shooting in the dark to a certain degree and will only know the really pertinent questions to ask when we are in the new world order. Even then, we will have to wait to see how all the unforeseen consequences play out over time. What we do know is that the RDR preparation and implementation journey is not a 'Y2K' issue. We are not faced with a set deadline where we'll all either self implode or absolutely nothing will change. We have a marathon ahead, not a sprint and one that needs all the careful planning and ingredients in place to ensure the best possible outcomes will be achieved.

So what could those outcomes look like?

1. Skin in the game: Those businesses that can have a vested interest in their staff and stakeholders and are aligned with RDR compliance will stand a better chance of sustainability.

2. Clarity on Value: Understanding the value chain and value propositions the business provides the consumer is imperative. This applies to restricted and independent advice channels, pricing of products and AC.

3. Partnership: Strategic alliances when wealth managers and IFAs join forces with other professional industries such as law firms and accountants will be of huge benefit. Banks may incorporate platforms and IFA services, platforms may see discretionary management services as an attractive offering for clients.

4. Innovation: All market participants to focus on best practice technology for clients, incorporating an easy to understand, client-generic interface keeping product and options straightforward.

5. Understanding: Knowing where the business sits in the industry is imperative and this applies not only to the UK but also Europe. The UK is leading regulatory change with the RDR, but the EU is following with the PRIPS framework that may have a tipping effect on the RDR.

6. Client first: Structuring the business interests around the clients' needs and wants seems simple, yet few companies truly employ such a strategy. Understanding the clients' objectives and their experiences with your services has never been more important and is now more varied dependent on where you sit within the market.

7. Efficiency: Streamlining the business model, knowing where resources are to be found and how the charges and fees are to be structured will ensure profitability and that a sustainable framework is in place.

 #RDRBOOK

Such outcomes will give the organisation the best possible chance of surviving through the RDR journey and coming out stronger and more versatile as the market takes its shape in 2013. Of course we do not know how the market will shape up, but we have good examples to call upon as potential guidance if needed. Australia's move to platform-based advice has been well documented. In the 1990s it had a similar RDR style transformation of its financial services driven by investors' needs for self-sufficiency. The simplification and market ethics focus of the regulators enabled the move from 'off-the-shelf' and 'one size fits all' products to transparent and sophisticated web-based 'wraps' or platforms. These were designed to streamline the investing and administration of individual, trust and company investment portfolios.

Figure 3.1: Selecting funds and wrappers in theory: the life product 'wrapper' model

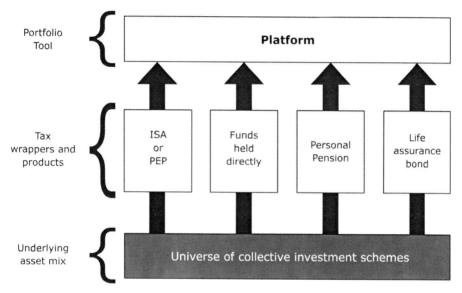

SOURCE: FSA DP 07/2 'Platforms: the role of wraps and fund supermarkets'.

Such a consolidated investment system through the internet gives a single 24-7 valuation system that traditionally had been scattered amongst a range of companies and products such as pensions, unit and investment trusts. Each with differing charging structures and full back office customer relationship management support (CRM).

This wrap style investment structure's aims of offering an all-encompassing solution have only been partially met in the Australian market. Additionally, with only three or four bank-operated platforms available, the possibilities of market dominance and a lack of competition, which can drive prices up for the consumers, have concerned the regulators. An example of such was the Competition Commission's rejection of the acquisition talks between NAB and AXA AP in September 2010.

Without getting too carried away with the world of wraps and platforms (as I devote a large part of Chapter 6 to this subject), it is important to note that the often-cited financial service market change in Australia is not without its own issues. Indeed true fee based advice does not quite exist as the RDR rules stipulate, yet a common theme between such regulatory driven market change can be seen in one word, transparency.

3.4 Transparency in Business

One of the most valiant principles of the original six RDR objectives was "an industry that engages with consumers in a way that delivers more clarity for them on products and services". This, added to the new principles of a transparent and fairer charging system, better qualification framework for advisers and greater clarity around the type of advice being offered, illustrates the strong emphasis on the need for transparency in RDR compliance.

The role of ethics has also gained importance in recent years as savvy consumers see through the attempts to hide things from them. What I mean by this is the public's demands for accountability in professional practice, whether in the public (e.g. MP's expenses scandal) or private (e.g. banking Payment Protection Insurance scandal - PPI) sectors. Getting the full value for what you have paid is now paramount and trust can surely only be delivered by an industry with full disclosure, not only of fees and charges but also of the value chain offered. The problem with this is quite simply there is a huge amount of information available to the consumer -just think about how many terms of business and products are bundled at present into SIPPS or ISAs for example.

So with RDR organisational change programmes running at full speed, I would argue that transparency across the business structure alongside communication in a clear and concise manner could facilitate trust and maintain client relations in a simple and efficient manner. What we need is a blueprint for transparency across all the essential processes involved in retail financial services. This needs to go beyond the competence and commission functions that the RDR is commonly misinterpreted as and aids the huge task of taking existing business models through the RDR implementation phase and into true fee based charging.

As an industry, financial services has been pretty good at disguising some inconvenient truths, particularly in relation to the real cost of products and services, and about the level of risk that to which some of these products and services expose the public. Much of this is not the fault of individuals, as a lot of the worst excesses have become institutional. Extra allocation rates, trail commission rebates, opaque layering of charges and a conspiracy of obfuscation about how much and how the industry earns money out of the investing public, serves to keep them in the dark. The complexity of the financial services industry, which requires the delivery value chain to be distributed amongst different business entities with each relying on the transparency of each other, makes it almost impossible for the client to figure-out just:

- Whom should they engage?
- What and who offers value for money?
- Are all parties' interests aligned or are there significant conflicts of interest?

So by embracing transparency at the core of the change management process and viewing the organisation through the eyes of the clients, a clear and accountable service model can be engaged and understood creating trust and loyalty both internally and externally.

Transparency will also aid the subjective relationships many organisations find so difficult to manage. While processes and documentation should be easy to design in a clearer and more comprehensible fashion, the spoken word (which often supports the documentation or process engaged) is a different arena. One of the main critiques of social science theory is that it relies on the subjective views of participants within the research process, this applies when we attempt to assess the impact of what is said to clients at all levels of the business. Assessing the transparency of business communication by engaging and maintaining client relations in a compliant and ethical manner is a solution.

As we will see later in Chapter 8 on adviser charging for example, if each interface of stakeholder and client engagement is managed in a transparent manner then all interested parties should understand the value the business provides.

3.5 Summary
Change of any sort can be a frightening prospect for human beings, but with a well-planned, co-ordinated approach, organisations may actually thrive on change. Just look at those financial institutions that gained during and post the recent financial crises, a mix of chance and opportunism was the making of Barclays Capital for example. With any change whether forced or not comes opportunity, but strategy needs to be tempered with ethics and transparent solutions;

1. Understanding and implementing organisational change theory can facilitate meeting of desired outcomes
2. Institutional Theory can act as a guide to the desired business model
3. Transparency in business acts as a blueprint for consumer engagement and support.

Case Study 1: IFA Change Process

Gold Alliance (UK) Limited is small IFA based in York turning over between 250K and 500K and has been in business more than 10 years.

Advisers 2 - 3 support staff. The business completed its transition to the use of Wrap Platforms 2008/2009 and introduced model portfolios 2009/2010.

Pre RDR Actions

Client Generation

Created communication plan to communicate fees to existing clients

Expanded the business by purchasing pure fee based business. This turned out to be an excellent deal, as not only did the business acquire a large number of clients who already understand the fee model. The portfolio had an exceptionally high amount of cash which will require investing.

Reviewed the marketing plan to create more focus on a fee paying target market

Developed a presentation for potential clients who have to pay fees, trustees, attorneys etc

Developed a seminar marketing system to attract new referrals.

Reviewed introducer agreements and ensure all introducers understand the implications of RDR

Client Engagement

Redefined the service offering

Created new Terms of Business to deal with recovery of unpaid adviser charges.

Converted services in support of existing trail commission into retainer agreements for on - going adviser charging.

Introduced "Dropbox" technology to share files and documents with clients

Advice Process

Reviewed the implication for the new definition of Independent Advice. Created a project to understand the likely gaps in existing product sourcing services.

Agreed with clients likely triggers for requiring further advice.
Re - engineered the advice process to eliminate unproductive time which would not be recovered by fees.

Created a Transparency project to review the level of transparency of major suppliers, culling those from the panel which did little to add to transparency.

Investment Process

Improved their portfolio advisory service and repriced to reflect value

Review basis of operation with discretionary managers

Admin & Servicing

Moved accounting to a client basis and away from provider as client.

Improved MI in relation to different types of Legacy trail i.e. protection renewal, designated investment based renewal, AMC priced trail, and fund based renewal

Analysed previous two years cash flow shape and compared to a projected post RDR shape

Segmented client base to discover a better understanding of clients who will pay fees.

Reviewed all existing terms with providers and start tracking the changes to come about after RDR

Conducted an analysis of remuneration to determine whether VAT exemptions continue to apply and introduced a VAT assessment record for each case.

Quality & Satisfaction

Introduced activity timing to get an accurate idea of the time taken to do regulated tasks

Updated TCF gap analysis

Redesigned post advice client feedback questionnaire to ensure clients can feedback on clarity of costs etc.

Chapter 4

Understanding the Value Chain

"The value chain is a systematic approach to examining the development of competitive advantage"
M E Porter 1980.

A value chain is a group of activities which when placed in a specific order define an organisation's operations in a specific industry. In our case the retail financial service value chain is of great interest to both the market participants and consumers alike.

If we understand the value chain, how it is connected and how it affects businesses, industry and consumers we begin to understand the key problems and challenges that the RDR change management process presents. Such study will also show clients how efficient its processes are and the businesses value in how it passes on costs to them.

There are two value chains that we can contemplate, one that I define as internal that affects the business model and the other is external and has a direct effect on the market and consumers.

4.1 Internal Value Chains

An example of a financial services relevant internal value chain is given in Figure 4.1. This model is based on the value chain first devised by social scientist Michael Porter in 1985. As a management tool, the value chain is extremely powerful for strategic planning. Each function of this value chain is inter and co-dependant and thus will need careful structuring and ongoing monitoring and management to ensure synergy, sustainability and profitability.

The value chain also acts as a business model in its own right to understand the interconnected structures that make up the organisation. Finally it helps to best understand the return on investment, costs and profitability of the business operations.

Why is this relevant? The financial services industry faces many challenges from the RDR and it is imperative that organisations carefully plan their internal structure to create fee based financial planning, product design and services that will ensure a sustainable business once it is in place.

Figure 4.1: The Internal Value Chain

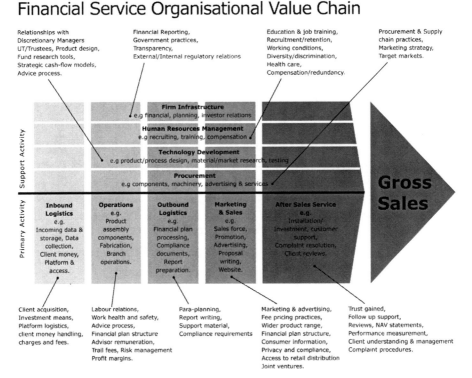

This diagram gives clear examples of how a retail financial services organisation may organise its internal functions to ensure synergy with key performance indicators. Split into two levels, the support activity covers all back office functions to ensure the offering is sound. The primary activity aligns all actions to attractive service offers, client procurement, retention and profitability of operations.

4.2 The External Value Chains

At present, the external retail investment value chain involves several agents (see Figure 4.2). These range from the fund manager, responsible for managing the underlying assets in a product portfolio, through to the product provider, packaging the portfolio in the most suitable form for a wide variety of investors. The intermediary is responsible for advising the ultimate purchaser on the suitability of the product to match their particular requirements. The same overall structure applies to both pure savings and investment products as well as those combining an insurance element with investments.

It is this value chain that begins to 'pass on' costs to the consumer and is of greatest interest post RDR compliance. It is clear that the external value chain, in relation to adviser charging, taxation of the business and individuals, investment management and technology to access financial products, plays a crucial role to the success of the organisation in the move to fee based advice.

Figure 4.2: The External Value Chain

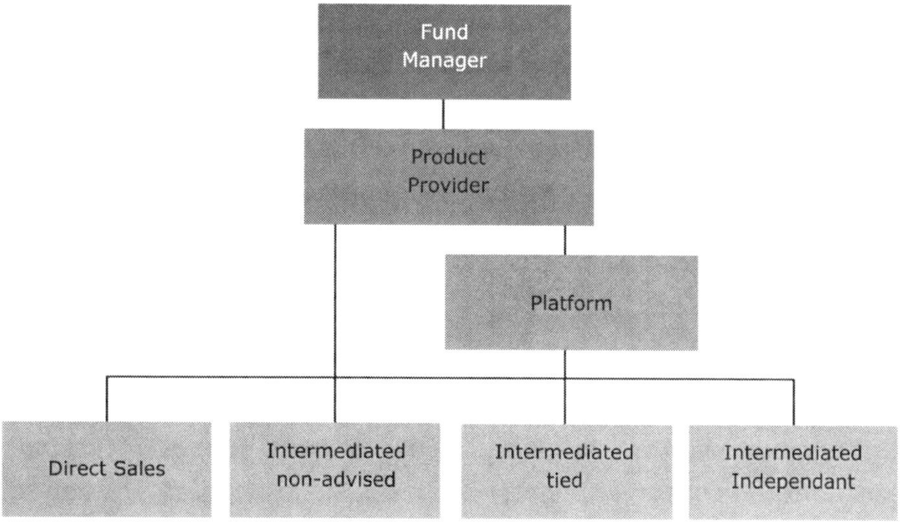

SOURCE: *Oxera Retail Distribution Review proposals: Impact on market structure and competition*[6] 🐦 #RDRBOOK

So let's take a look at the key areas of this value chain:

Fund Manager

Costs will arise at all stages along the chain, beginning with the fund manager who will incur dealing and administration costs for the portfolio on which the retail product is based. It is not straightforward to isolate these particular costs because managers generally combine the assets in a range of funds, both retail and wholesale, that they have under management. The costs of this fund management will be passed on to the product provider in the form of management fees.

Retail Fund and Product Providers

The product provider is responsible for allocating the assets to a particular (retail) fund and packaging this fund in the most appropriate form. Costs will be incurred in structuring the fund and in its ongoing administration. In addition, the provider will incur costs in supporting the distribution of the product, which it may undertake itself or through an intermediary such as a financial adviser.

Many retail fund providers use their in-house management operations to undertake such activity. As a result, it can be difficult to separate the costs of this activity from those incurred in providing a retail product that is in the most suitable form for the consumer. This alone illustrates the difficult nature of ensuring transparency for the consumer and needs to be addressed by the regulators as well as all interested market participants to ensure product charges are fair and clear.

In the new world of fee based advice, asymmetry needs to be avoided and fund and product providers should be forced to ensure all charges are disclosed including those that are passed on by a third party, e.g. wrap or platform providers. Similarly cross subsidising cannot exist and the consumer should, in theory, be in a strong position to

[6] *Oxera; Retail Distribution Review proposals: Impact on market structure and comptetition. Prepared for the FSA June 2009*

demand a transparent and fairly priced service that also allows the market to thrive and compete.

Platforms and Wraps

The development of platforms has reduced the potential administration costs incurred by advisers. These largely online services enable the adviser to screen investments on offer more efficiently, as well as enabling a more holistic approach to be taken to the management of a client portfolio.

Again it is imperative for the consumer that full charges are disclosed by platform and wrap providers and there are no rebates payments made available as per FSA directives. The regulators also need to be vigilant in ensuring that such platforms take a clear stance on the bundling/unbundling issues we discussed in the previous chapter. If platforms and wraps are to survive in the RDR world then they should unravel all charges and thus bundling becomes only an unavoidable necessity.

Financial Advisers

Figure 4.3: Financial adviser workflow value chain

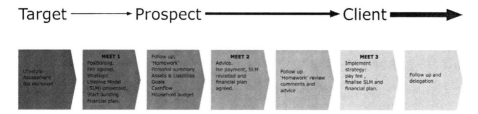

SOURCE: Engage Partnership Ltd; RDR advice workflow.

 #RDRBOOK

As we have seen, the RDR enforces professionalism across all financial adviser activities. An adviser's costs will arise mainly from marketing; prospecting for, and negotiating with, potential customers and providing the advice that is given before the consumer makes the final purchase. Knowledge of the product markets is paramount and this information needs to be updated regularly.

They need to comply with regulatory requirements to ensure that the purchaser is provided with adequate and appropriate information in order to make a suitable choice. These requirements will involve the 'lifestyle assessment' or needs analysis where the client's circumstances and investment needs are discussed before a recommendation is made. A financial plan on suitable products must then be provided, including an indication of potential risks and returns according to standardised regulatory requirements.

The adviser must provide documentation post-purchase to confirm their assessment of the client's circumstances and the appropriateness of the product recommended. In the case of certain retail products (e.g. company pensions), the adviser may also need to monitor the product and provide updated advice as necessary on an ongoing basis. At all stages, for regulatory purposes, the adviser must ensure that records are kept of the advice given and the transactions undertaken.

If the adviser is part of a network, some of the compliance activity and administration of the client's assets may be undertaken centrally i.e. outsourced where more costs may prevail.

4.3 Investment Value Chain

Costs in the present structure for the wealth management industry value chain are detailed in Figure 4.4. This shows the total approximate cost of investment to the client whatever the investment platform and fund type used. Although generalist in nature, this information is essential when considering the need for transparency and fairness in costs and remuneration that the RDR stipulates.

Figure 4.4: Investment Value Chain

Asset Management and other products	Product Design	Dealership	Adviser Practices	Advisers	Clients
50-70 Bps	70-90 Bps	5-15 Bps	50-70 Bps	40-60 Bps	

Total (Approx) 250Bps + Inflation

SOURCE: *Macquarie Financial Services Group.*

 #RDRBOOK

Figure 4.4 clearly illustrates the Total Expense Ration (TER) when money flows through the investment value chain, currently with an inflation lag of approximately 3%+. This means that the total cost to the consumer is as much as 5.5%+pa before they are in a position to enjoy a real return from their investment. I believe this is a conservative estimation, particularly as we're now experiencing higher inflation levels.

This effectively means (where the investment value chain is concerned) that the discretionary fund manager needs to add a huge amount of value before the investor sees real return on their investment.

Such an unbalanced system means that consumers have already become distrustful of the financial services industry and this problem is one that now must be addressed where RDR compliance is concerned.

Return On Investment: ROI - Effect of Inflation

A return may be adjusted for inflation to better indicate its true value in purchasing power. Any investment with a nominal rate of return less than the annual inflation rate represents a loss of value, even though the nominal rate of return might well be greater than 0 percent.

When ROI is adjusted for inflation, the resulting return is considered an increase or decrease in purchasing power. If an ROI value is adjusted for inflation, it is stated explicitly, such as "The return, adjusted for inflation was 2 percent".

The move to transparent fee based advising gives an opportunity for all parties in the value chain to address any confusion and mistrust the industry has fairly or unfairly garnered. It should ensure that once and for all the client feels empowered by the knowledge of what the advice and the investment value chain they enter is actually costing in real terms.

This 'trusted' status will be reflected by revealing the value chain internal expense ratio that lies beneath the surface. Indeed, the effects of taxation on the return on investment must also be properly stated, leaving the consumer with fair information to consider before an investment should be made.

Taxation
The final piece in the value chain jigsaw is that of taxation and a big question for any financial services organisation's value chain is one of return on investment. The effect of inflation and taxation on the consumer and the product purchased are firmly associated with this, but sometimes conveniently forgotten.

We know the financial services industry is facing an unprecedented challenge to show fair value through the internal and external value chain of services or products, yet this is compromised by charges and also the effect of taxation along the chain.

One key area is the taxation of insurance companies through the Income minus Expense (I-E) system. With the exception of pensions, life companies receive various forms of tax relief on their charges because under the commission regime they sit within the relievable expenses. In theory such 'discounts' were being passed on by lower product charges. Despite the changes in the April '11 budget, which effectively removes tax relief from expenses, it is still unclear how this will affect adviser charging, but it is difficult to see how under current taxation, legislation and the budget changes, that such tax relief could be anything other than moved out of life company expenses.

This adds a potential double blow to the consumer who will no longer enjoy the tax relief passed on as lower charges and is likely to be charged VAT into the bargain. Just the thing for encouraging savings! We explore this further in Chapter 8.

This quite simply remains unaccounted for by the FSA's RDR proposals and may have intangible ramifications on both product and adviser charging.

4.4 Evidence Based Management (EBM)

Evidence-Based Practice:

- Learning about cause-effect connections in professional practices
- Isolating the variations that measurably affect desired outcomes
- Creating a culture of evidence-based decision-making and research participation
- Using information-sharing communities to reduce over-use, under-use and misuse of specific practices
- Building decision-supports to promote practices that the evidence validates, along with techniques and artefacts that make the decision easier to execute or perform (e.g. checklists and protocols)
- Having individual, organisational and institutional factors promote access to knowledge and its use

Denise M. Rousseau 2005

So what can the business value chain and associated entities provide us with when we focus on the RDR challenges and opportunities?

Firstly the key issues surrounding mystification and unintended consequences can be met head on by close analysis of the data alongside the implicit and explicit relationships that the value chains provide us. By quantifying the RDR change impact with value chain analysis, we can assess whether the actions taken to address such change is appropriate or not. As an analogy, if we still believed the world was flat and based our everyday planning around this assumption, the world would be a very different place than it is today. As Columbus found, we need to explore to find empirical evidence to provide better knowledge to understand exactly what any landscape may actually look like. Where the RDR is concerned we need to know if the value chain and business models in place are appropriate or not.

Using EBM on the value chain is essentially analysing the efficiency and effectiveness of business operations, mitigating and reducing risks associated with changes that need to be made or the cause and effect of any outcomes whether change is made or not. The key is transparency when investigating the data and using this as a resource and guide for the broader context of the change programme. As we have seen in the preceding chapter, change management programmes need to be carefully managed, but with EBM at the heart of the change and the streamlining of the value chain, then the RDR principles can be applied with greater confidence.

All problems that will arise with any change to the business value chain or model will be around resistance to change such as availability of the data, capacity for change, a blame culture and an inability to think critically through the process. EBM is not a panacea by any means, but where the value chain is concerned it will offer a guide to the long-term impact that RDR change brings. As Rob Briner, Professor of Organisational Psychology at Birkbeck university recommends, when change is applied we need to ask: ***"Do we think this is true or do we know this is true?"*** to avoid catastrophic problems caused by incorrect changes the organisations and to the value chain.

4.5 Summary

As we investigate the internal and external value chains we begin to understand the complexities and interconnectivity that makes up the full operations of business and their impact on markets and consumers. It is through such value chain analysis that we'll understand how organisations may begin to re-structure their operations to meet RDR requirements. Their careful selection of charging and fee structures, product selection and service offering will mean either efficient RDR survival or extinction.

- Using Business Process Modelling map out the internal and external value chain, ensuring that key data regarding relationships, business processes and return on investment are factored and recorded.
- Ensure all factors are taken into account such as the affect of inflation and taxation.
- Start with the end outcome you wish to achieve and work backwards to assess the changes that are necessary.
- Use Evidence Based Management as a guide to ask the important questions and ensure high analytical literacy so that the business model and value chains are understood.

Chapter 5:

Behavioural Economics

"Success is 80% psychology and 20% mechanics"
Anthony Robbins.

It's about the clients, stupid! OR IS IT? Without their clients - banks, IFAs, Life companies, wealth managers and stockbrokers would be out of business. So they should make it their business to know their clients inside and out. We now live in an era where the psychology of the buyer, or in this case investor, is becoming more and more important to understand from both a retail and regulatory position.

For some time it has been acknowledged that the psychological attributes of the general public need to be understood if we want them to take ownership of their financial and future planning. This would ensure that value chains, products and regulation would be designed around consumer relationships with their finances. Behavioural economics is therefore essential as it studies the questions standard economics considers, but without the assumption that human beings are rational. It asks how people behave in connection with their finances and whether this is good or bad for them.

5.1 Regulation of Behaviour

Even before the UK Welfare State was created, politicians and economists were aware of the need to have systems and processes that forced the public to save and contribute for the welfare of themselves and future generations. In 1911 David Lloyd George suggested that national insurance contributions should benefit those in unemployment or ill health.

A century later nothing has changed, we now see the need for government and regulators alike to ensure company pension schemes involve compulsory contribution from both the pension member and (if they are lucky) their employer. The National Employment Savings Trust (NEST) pension auto-enrol initiative, endowment savings schemes with automatic premium escalation and, of course, national insurance contributions are still a necessity. With the implementation of the RDR we have a repricing of the industry and an unprecedented opportunity to ensure that the general public is comprehensively educated on the importance of financial planning. This will need the financial service industry to be finally weaned off its dependence on opaque product charging and commission based remuneration.

Nudge Policy

In their book 'Nudge', Thaler and Sunstein[7] advocate the benefits of 'libertararian paternalism'. This phrase is born from Milton Freidman's view that people should be free to choose, but they should have 'choice architects' who try and influence their behaviour in order to make their lives better, healthier and longer. If we lose any preconceived ideas regarding such philosophy, we may begin to see that any influence either from industry, government or regulator, if well intended and positioned, may be of great benefit to the client.

Communicate the value chain;

- Give clients full knowledge of your value
- Educate on the worth of your service
- Allow clients to evaluate their best buy options

Within financial services and with the RDR focus on consumer bias, nudge policy is one method for companies to engage in a healthy manner with their clients to ensure product or service features and benefits are designed around the customers' needs.

There is no doubt that this theory gives a huge opportunity for product designers in particular to move away from products for profit to those that include the features needed to encourage investment

[7] Thaler Richard H and Sunstein Cass R. 2009. Nudge, Improving decisions about health, wealth and happiness. *Penguin Books*. 1-295.

and planning to benefit and aid the clients capabilities. Surely this will also benefit the product providers themselves?

Barclays Wealth has conducted some excellent work in the impact of behavioural finance on product design. Greg Davies who heads up the Barclays behavioural finance and investment philosophy team mentions that the commercial applications for behavioural science within product design is an exciting up and coming arena one that needs to be strongly encouraged.[8]

A good example of how this may work from a regulatory point of view is full communication and transparency of the value chain detailed in the last chapter. This will ensure that consumers understand the full value to them of services rendered and be educated on why it would be beneficial for them to invest.

Thaler and Sunstein call this type of disclosure 'RECAP' - Record, Evaluate, and Compare Alternate Prices - which aims to educate clients on all forms of product pricing. Producing RECAP reports (a form of buyer's guides) may actually engage clients by informing and educating on pricing of the value chain. In parallel it can encourage industry development of third party services that compare prices over the internet, a subject we will cover in Chapter 10 on technological innovation. An example of bad practice from another industry is mobile phone contract terms and conditions. It's now becoming impossible for the consumer to actually decipher if they are receiving true value in minutes used on the contract they sign up for thanks to pages of minutiae and detail, probably designed to put off the examination of the contract in the first place.

As I'm sure we all know: the devil's in the detail. Just take a moment and think about how many terms of business and fund prospectuses there are in the investment value chain (e.g. purchase of investments

[8] Barclays Wealth Insights: Volume 13: Risk and Rules the role of control in financial decision-making. June 2011.

through a SIPP platform). If a consumer has full access to all this information in a simplified 'buyer's guide' then surely they will begin to understand exactly what they are paying for and aid the choice for purchase.

It is worth noting that the EU Key Investment Information Documents (KIID) may have a spill over into the RDR.

5.2 Importance of Psychology

Sigmund Freud and Karl Jung, the two most revered psychologists of the last century believed in varying degrees that human beings were essentially driven by their ego and related self-interest. Indeed when we drill down into the world of psychoanalysis, we discover numerous theories that help when attempting to understand why people do what they do in relation to their finances.

- The psychological contract discusses a mutual belief or perception based give and get exchange which, for example sets the dynamic for the relationship between employee and employer or in our case, client and financial company
- Attachment theory describes infant attachment styles to parental figures: security, anxious and avoidant, which describe underlying psychological motivations or views (unmet needs, attachment needs). E.g. two individuals faced with the same financial challenge may approach investment in very different ways
- Baseline mental-health considers personality measures as reflections of well being. Certain personality types e.g. for those who score high towards a neurotic approach, their 'baseline' for a pessimistic view will be higher than those with a more constructive personality style. This can effect financial capability and provide some answers as to why disposition is important in making financial decisions.

Yet whatever theory we decide to apply, if default and nudge style policy can work, why do we still have a position where only 1/3rd of the UK working population actually contributes to a pension and more than 13.5 million remain in poverty at retirement?

Critics of the RDR point to the fact that it is designed with far too much regulatory stick and not enough carrot for the industry to align its services to place clients' needs first and so understand behavioural finance. As we have seen with the 'default and nudge' policy,

Behavioural Economics Defined

"people's financial behaviour may primarily depend on their intrinsic psychological attributes rather than information or skills or how they choose to deploy them".

David de Meza et al, FSA Consumer research paper 69.

government and regulators may employ as much paternal libertarianism as they like, but at the end of the day it is still the client who has to choose to invest and plan for their financial future.

In their consultation paper to the FSA, David de Meza et al make a solid case for understanding behavioural economics. The main thrust of this paper is that we should improve the financial capability of the general public in five key areas: 1) Managing money 2) Planning ahead 3) Choosing products 4) Staying informed and 5) Making ends meet. 🐦 #RDRBOOK

As the RDR places the bias on the client then the above five strategies must be researched and understood by any organisation affected. The reason? Plain and simple (as we have found) the general public have become far more discerning than they were in the past, for reasons such as the recent credit crunch. We only have to look at the UK Members of Parliament (MPs) expenses scandal, banks mis-selling of PPI and recent phone hacking scandals to see that transparency means not only release of information and accountability, but also an understanding of the audience affected by such behaviour.

In retail financial services terms this means a complete understanding of the important role this industry has in supporting the education, decision-making skills and general betterment of consumers' financial planning techniques. In this sense the RDR brings a great opportunity for business to fearlessly engage and maintain client relations through efficient and transparent communication and service.

To understand how business should employ psychological based strategies and, maybe more importantly, take on a corporate responsibility for educating and engaging the general public we refer back to David de Meza and his colleagues who make a very strong argument for psychological factors in financial capability. In their paper they emphasise that while industry information is important to convey to the consumer, it's the cognitive process that is essential and often overlooked. Disposition, procrastination, inertia, buyer's remorse, loss aversion, mental accounting, status quo bias, overconfidence and information overload all have a major psychological impact on the consumer. In other words, de Meza and others recognise that financial capability does not necessarily lead to economically rational behaviour. Indeed their paper predicts the financial capability agenda will not succeed alone. This is based on their findings that:

- Consumers are not economically rational
- They do not respond to price signals
- They are not discerning buyers of financial services
- Default or nudge strategies are more likely to succeed
- Adviser charging will only succeed in the higher net worth market

5.3 The Human Brain and Cognitive Activity

Until recently, issues surrounding financial capability such as investment decision making have been influenced by financial economics rather than from a psychological stance. Yet with empirical work undertaken by social scientists such as Richard Thaler, we now see compelling evidence that human psychology and the cognitive workings of the brain play an integral role in financial capability. In fact, it offers an explanation why both industry and the consumer are continuously found wanting on financial stability.

With this in mind, it's worth taking a look at the science behind the mental activity associated with financial capability. In his book 'Flipnosis'[9] Dr Kevin Dutton describes the psychological process of instant influence techniques most commonly used by politicians, advertisers, salesmen and, yes, functional psychopaths that if used correctly can seal a deal instantly. Ethics is obviously an important ingredient here!

Kamstra, Kramer, and Levi (2003):

Present international evidence that seasonal depression, which correlates with the length of the day, has a negative effect on stock returns.

An important point to note here is a social science term called heuristics. This is experienced based techniques used for problem solving. With heuristic activity, the brain uses such experience as a 'guide' through decision-making processes to better enable the perceived desired outcome to be reached. Dutton says;

"(Brains) are slothful creatures of habit. Rather than preparing decisions from scratch using fresh, seasonal ingredients, they prefer the ready-made variety - chock-full of conjecture, assumption and pre-packaged, freeze-dried reasoning."

Indeed Dutton goes as far as suggesting that functional psychopaths, people who can almost ruthlessly separate emotion from action, can make excellent investors i.e. fear of loss does not come into play.

Such views on human nature and cognitive abilities go back to the Ancient Greek philosophers; Plato, Aristotle and Socrates who specifically described human nature as two horses - one of reason and one of irrational behaviour - commanded by a charioteer. We can thus see emotion and rationality as opposites that for some people are a financial recipe for disaster.

[9] Dutton David. 2010. Flipnosis, The Art of Split-Second Persuasion. *Arrow Books*. 1-381

Neuroscience shows examples of decision making governed by both the affective and cognitive regions of the brain, where the affective (limbic) region, designed for survival and reproduction, is generally overridden by the cognitive activity. Gambling, risk taking or procrastination and inertia for example can be a result of the limbic region gaining control due to the desire for instant gratification. The term 'neuroeconomics' describes the cognitive decision making processes that drive financial decisions and thus is governed by limbic and cognitive factors.

5.4 Systematic Biases

Judgemental biases are a good way for us to understand these cognitive complexities in action. As reported in de Meza's paper there are key decision making processes and biases that affect people's relations with their finances and it's worth noting the most salient concepts that can contribute to a tendency to certain beliefs:

- Disposition: Openness, Conscientiousness, Agreeableness, Extroversion, Neuroticism (OCEAN) represent the big five character traits as devised by Lewis Goldberg[10] in 1990. How others perceive us is dependent on how we display to them. Therefore a financial judgment made when we are conscientious, agreeable and open rather than sceptical, anxious and unconfident will enhance our financial awareness, capacity and help us relate to our financial goals.

  Yet we see time and time again individuals and organisations selling stocks too early or buying too late on the investment cycle i.e. the investment is sold early before significant gains are made and investments made when to asset is riding high at the top of the cycle as charted below.

---

[10] Goldberg Lewis R. 1990. An Alternative "Description of personality": The BIG-FIVE factor structure.Journal of Personality and Social Psychology, Vol 59(6) 1216-1229.

Chart 5.1: Mistiming the investment cycle.

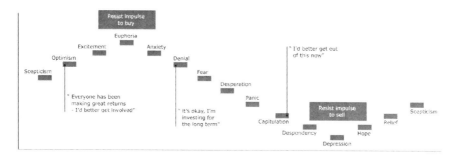

SOURCE: *Barclays Wealth Insights Volume 13: Risk and Rules The role of control in financial decision-making.*

- <u>Overconfidence and control illusion:</u> I'm sure many people will attribute these concepts to the stereotypical stock trader or banker. Yet it is true to say that we all suffer from time to time from becoming overconfident in our finances. It is part of the human condition to try and ensure control over events, particularly chance events such as market movements. 'Hindsight bias' is an example where we assume we know more than we do.

Julian B Rotter's theory of *'locus of control'* [11] is of interest in relation to consumer confidence and perceived control. This refers to the extent individuals believe they may control events that affect them. So in financial terms individuals with a high internal locus of control believe that they are responsible for their financial success or failure. Alternatively those with low internal locus of control (i.e. external) believe significant others, markets, regulators or fate play the major role in determining their financial situation.

Tied into Rotter's theory is Martin Seligmans 'learned helplesness'[12] which explains feelings of resignation and lack of caring in one's fate. This can explain why individuals

[11] *Rotter, J. B. (1954) Social learning and clinical psychology. New York: Prentice Hall.*
[12] *Seligman, M. M.E.P (1975) Helplessness:on depression, development and death*

become depressed and resigned if they lose money or have a negative experience with financial services firms. Lee Ross' 'fundamental attribution error'[13] also fits in with control illusions. This describes the human tendency to overvalue dispositional or personality based explanations for behaviour rather than situational explanations. An example is individuals being blamed for certain events rather than the overall situational context: 'Banker bashing' gone crazy?

- Gender: A tricky ground for some but (sorry gents) there are studies that show women make sounder financial judgements than men. A recent study by Barclays and Ledbury Research found that women were more likely to make money as investors in the financial markets. This is due to women's greater self-control and lower over-confidence, which leads to caution. Women tend to be anticipatory, questioning and self-depreciating in their approach compared to men's rather more aggressive and direct tactics.

- Mental accounting: Evaluation, organising and keeping track of household and individual financial activities. The human mind seems to only have a few ways of dealing with such methods and has great difficulty in closing such accounts at a loss.

- Loss aversion: Greed and fear, the experience of losing money is felt far more intensely and negatively than any gains made. The term myopic risk aversion is used to describe losses being experienced in isolation thus felt harder.

- Hedonic editing: In creating mental accounts and with loss aversion in mind, people will separate gains and integrate losses to maximize happiness.

- Hyperbolic discounting: This alludes to the fact that people prefer the short term to long term planning. For example we tend to want short-term rewards and thus discount the value of the later reward despite its benefits.

- Status Quo bias: Human beings do not like change. This means that where finances are concerned anything that can create a

---

[13] *Ross, L. (1991): The person and the situation; Persepectives of social psychology: New York; McGraw-Hill*

negative change is felt far harder than a positive change. The 'endowment effect' is an example where we value goods far more when we own them than when we do not. We tend to follow the path of least resistance which ties up with myopic activity, i.e. seeing risks in isolation and as above, hyperbolic discounting, choosing less painful options in the short term which may not be helpful in the long term.[14]

- Relativity: Most people don't know exactly what they want until they see it in context. For example, when purchasing an investment individuals like to see benchmarks such as the 'efficiency frontier' detailed later in Chapter 10, which shows the return gained for the risk taken gives an idea of the type of investing that may suit our needs. Tied in with this is 'anchoring' where a set price (e.g. cost) may be given by a firm and thus gives a context for discussion around charging.

- Inertia and Procrastination: In his book 'predictably irrational'[15] Dan Ariely gives a great example of how to manage his student's inertia. His students are tasked with 3 assignments over a semester where one group is allowed to hand in each assignment whenever they wish, a second group set there own deadlines and third have set staggered deadlines. The caveat is that there is a 1% penalty if handed in after the semester. The group that gave the best marks were those with the set deadline, the worst.... you guessed it, the ones with complete freedom, hence why defaults are favoured by regulators and governments alike.
#RDRBOOK

The above range of rather extreme viewpoints are tempered by Herbert Simon's 'bounded rationality' that states in general individuals do the best they can with the information and decision-making ability that is available. This is an example of how decision-making is limited by the available information at hand rather than expansive research taken.

---

[14] *Product providers across industries rely on client procrastination and inertia i.e. client 'loyalty' can be based on a lack of energy or enthusiasm to challenge the status quo.*
[15] *Arierly Dan 2009 Predictably Irrational. Harper Collins 1-353*

Simon's opinion that humans are only partly rational and mainly emotional/irrational concurs with de Meza's view on the irrational mind's control of consumers' financial capability. Although a slightly bizarre and uncomfortable truth, once we have recognised this and most importantly accepted it we can do something constructive about it.

5.5 Possible solutions

So how can the industry pick up on such psychological traits, propensities and behaviour to enable a consumer friendly service to be offered which will facilitate a trusted client relationship.

1. Education:

While there are plenty of companies that currently offer excellent education to the investor on their products, services and market place, this is not enough for the RDR.

We need to see more engagement with clients to encourage understanding in the very structure of the procurement of services (value chains). This will ensure clients understand the business model and how it affects them (in a positive way) during their investment and financial planning lives.

We are seeing good work by the Financial Education and Curriculum Inquiry that is currently suggesting ways to transform financial education in schools to establish a consistent and sustainable model. The All Party Parliamentary Group (APPG) led by Andrew Percy MP will lead this inquiry at government level with the emphasis on enhancing the financial education and capability of school children.

Web based educational sites have also appeared with moneysupermarket.com, moneysavingsexpert.com and allmyplans. com three examples of consumer centred websites for increasing awareness and capability.

However, examples such as the Skipton Building Society's research that winning the National Lottery is considered a significant part of the financial planning process for one in seven Yorkshire residents. Or the FSA's findings that 9 percent of tenants buy buildings' insurance on the property they live in despite the fact it's only the landlords who can claim. It's apparent there is still much to do to better inform and educate the consumer in financial capability.

Indeed immersive games are now being tested by the pan-European project xdelia to test whether innovative techniques using 'serious games' that use gaming technology, such as interactive simulation, can test and improve the public's financial capabilities.

2. Compliance:
Rules and better information on product marketing that create a 'buyer's mood' need to be adopted so the consumer can begin to trust the industry once again and realise that salesmanship is being tempered with a realistic compliant approach. This may involve restricting the choice of products being offered to avoid information overload, commitment devices such as group savings schemes (e.g. Rotating Savings and Credit Associations and Christmas clubs) and encouraging engagement and action on all the advice offered.

A Self-Regulatory Nudge?

An American who was addicted to gambling decided to take out an injunction against himself entailing he would be arrested upon entering any casino.

Thaler & Sunstein: Nudge

The advantages of limited choice are shown by social science experiments such as the famous 'Jam experiment'[16] conducted by Sheena Iyengar and Mark Lepper in 2000. They set up tasting booths and displayed either six or twenty four samples of jam to passers-by,

---

[16] Ivyenger Sheena, Lepper Mark, Journal of Personality and Social Psychology, Vol (79) 2000.

40 percent stopped for the six and 60 percent for the twenty four, but only 3 percent bought from the latter and a huge 30 percent from the limited display.

3. Defaults, nudges and regulation:
It's often said people are more likely to divorce their spouse than their bank manager! If financial organisations simplify their value chains, encourage financial education of the public and welcome realistic regulation to protect people from themselves it might stop financial inertia. This is a psychological trait credit card companies, insurance and banks 'rely' upon to make their money through offering teasers to gain customers and then keep them through the customer's own inertia. For example as stipulated in the introduction, a nil percent initial offer from a credit card draws people in, but they don't then move when that introductory rate increases.

Conversely defaults also work due to inertia for example compulsory enrolment in a UK superannuation pension scheme usually means once a person joins they are unlikely to leave. However, if there were originally offered a choice whether to join or not some would stay out.

The House of Lords Science and Technology Committee headed by Baroness Neuberger have produced a comprehensive report[17] on behavioural change intervention and conclude that nudge policy works best when allied with regulation and fiscal measures. This may ask questions of the Big Society agenda which seems to just rely on nudging alone.

4. Lifestyle Assessment models:
There is now a move towards encouraging mental accounting via household budget planning: envisioning the trade off's that need to be made and clients' relationship with their money. This is encouraging to

[17] House of Lords Science and Technology Select Committee, 2011 Behavioural Change Report 1-111

see and certainly cash-flow analysis technology is now available from providers to help clients interact in a positive way when managing their financial affairs.

5. Managing change:
It's fair to say human beings do not like change, yet change is a natural part of life in general and as the recent financial crises has illustrated, those organisations that demonstrate adaptability are those that strengthen. Yet with such market dynamics it is the consumer (or the taxpayer) who is affected and industry in general needs to learn that, without the consumer, they will not be in business.

Maintaining the status quo can be important to individuals, yet companies can play a significant role in ensuring that clients do not rest on their laurels and are carefully lifted out of their comfort zones for their financial betterment. Strategies involving face-to-face financial advice, product development with deadline and default options and simplified information will help.

6. Improving financial capability:
The FSA baseline theory was introduced to help with cognitive bias and simplify the decision making process involved in investing and financial planning. This involved recommendations around:
- Hindsight bias - assuming we know more than we do i.e. recognising overconfidence.
- Planning fallacy - underestimation of a task to completion.
- Financial education - aiding better decision-making.
- Escalation fallacy - avoiding throwing good money after bad.
- Anchoring effect - influence of previously considered experience or price (e.g. benchmarking fee based financial planning at realistic and affordable levels)
- Subjective judgments - emotion laden judgements affects risk evaluation.

So if we now begin to take into account individual's experience with financial services (known as a heuristically based decision process) we can then improve financial capability. Seen through Max Bazerman's 2008 work[18], three areas can then be judged;

1. Improving availability of information - Through memory enhancement, education and transparency.

2. Understanding 'Representativeness' - understanding stereotyping of the industry i.e. people tend to look for characteristics of a company, individual or situation based on previously formed views. E.g. names given to bankers post the credit crunch 'banksters'.

3. Managing the 'anchoring' and 'affect heuristic' - acknowledging judgments maybe influenced by subjective feelings such as emotionally laden judgments (negative affect i.e. anger, sadness or disgust at a financial loss).

This means that clients need help when it comes to managing their financial affairs with industry acknowledgement of Bazerman's 3 issues and thus engaging clients with information and services that will aid long term planning, instill discipline and stop 'knee-jerk' reactions to market movements. Similarly, the industry itself also needs to ensure blinkered (myopic) and short term goal attainment (hyperbolic discounting) are managed, which will reduce risk for all in creating sustainability in rational and calm approach to managing crises and change.

7. Simplification

The phrase 'keep it simple, stupid' applies right across the topics discussed in this book. Transparency of communication, investment options, charges, costs, fees, features and benefits of products options will reduce ambiguity and any perceived confusion and complexity by clients. This encourages engagement rather than procrastination and other aversive biases we have discussed. Simple product and simplified advice anyone?

 #RDRBOOK

---

[18] *Bazerman, Max, Katherine Milkman and Dolly Chugh How can decision-making be improved?*

Debiasing techniques may then be employed such as considering the contrarian or opposite view, improving accountability, cooling off periods, training in rules and representations, emotional regulation strategies and finally the affect of group decisions. As the credit crunch has shown, if we can begin to learn to see the wider picture, be critical in our acceptance of information and take more responsibility for decisions we can strengthen the financial capability of clients. Especially if this is taken alongside recognising the 'follow the herd' mentality and realising engagement in financial planning is a two way process.

8. Leave it to the fairer sex:

In his book, "Man down: proof beyond reasonable doubt that women are better cops, drivers, gamblers, spies, world leaders, beer tasters, hedge fund managers and just about anything else", Dan Abram's[19] research presents the case for women in the fact that men tend to get carried away by impulses such as ego, pride, over-confidence. There is certainly the case for more women to be in the boardroom and in control of financial institutions as we attempt to improve financial capabilities.

9. Culture shift:

A masculine culture tends to permeate many industries, where quick, brash decision making is expected. Yet according to some linguistic and behavioural experts, anticipatory questioning and a counter-intuitive approach leads to better results. Sometimes sleeping on decisions can yield better longer terms results.

So De Meza's paper, the Thorenson Report[20] submitted to the government in 2008, the FSA baseline report and the APPG's focus on the education of school children in financial capability are examples

---

[19] Abrams Dan. 2011 Man Down: Proof beyond reasonable doubt that women are better cops, drivers, gamblers, spies, world leaders, beer tasters, hedge fund managers and just about anything else. Abrams Books, 1-144.
[20] Thorenson Otto. 2008 Thorenson Review of generic financial advice: final report. 1-98.

of the governing body listening to behavioural economics and social science examination of financial capability. To me it seems quite clear that where the RDR is concerned, we need to keep an open mind as to what the best form of regulatory strategy is to encourage a better understanding of the psychology involved in investments and managing financial matters.

5.6 Summary

Behavioural finance and economics has only recently become a real policy influencing strategy after years of availability and research. This could be down to the fact that policy makers and regulators have been sceptical when it comes to social science and the wiring of the mind. However, if instigated with integrity, it is pleasing to see governmental initiatives starting to incorporate behavioural concepts such as nudge style policy based on consumer behaviour with the longer term view of the betterment of their financial capability.

- Know thyself: It is important for all market participants i.e. not just clients (stupid) to understand the reasons behind EBP's cause and affect principle when applied to behavioural economics. Regulators, businesses and the consumers would be better placed to interact constructively if this was the case.
- Remember the 80/20 rule: Successful product placement and wealth management of financial planning is 80 percent psychology and 20 percent mechanics.
- Identify the nudges that can add value such as default options on pensions.
- Implement or engage in any financial education programmes that may be of benefit to both business and the consumers.
- Keep it simple, stupid.

Chapter 6:

Creating the Sustainable Business Model

"... all too often, a successful new business model becomes the business model for companies not creative enough to invent their own".

Gary Hamel.

In the first chapter we discussed the major challenges that offer both an opportunity and a risk to retail financial services. There is no doubt that one of the biggest challenges is getting the business model right and largest risks is getting it wrong, all the while trying to incorporate unforeseen consequences.

If we take a look at individual organisations affected by the RDR we will see unique and common challenges, which if met and managed will mean the difference between success and failure when complying with the new rules.

6.1 Independent Financial Advisers (IFAs), Wealth Managers and Banks

There are many opportunities available to financial organisations who aim to monopolise the ground post RDR implementation.

An IFA is a company that advises clients on all 'relevant market' issues. A relevant market is essentially all financial products and opportunities that meets the consumer's needs.

There are those amongst the financial services community who believe the RDR is actually an attempt to stop the majority of the public accessing IFAs . With potential polarisation of the industry as detailed in Chapter 1, (Independent advice affordable to HNW clients only), then we can see that the IFA industry is seriously challenged by the RDR.

The RDR leaves IFAs with two options:
i) *Independence:* One of the aims of the RDR is to let the consumer pay for advice on the 'whole of the market'. This basically means a fully holistic service incorporating technical tools, research capability and fully independent 'gold standard' advice.

In essence one would assume clients would want a fully independent approach where all aspects of a relevant market were considered when planning financially. Yet with the RDR requirements comes a quandary for IFAs. Will a fully independent service be too expensive to run? A good honest root and branch review is needed to assess if independence (however desirable) is actually a realistic option. This will include a view taken on the services offered by the IFA, such as:

- Has the client bank been assessed for suitability of independent services? (Client segmentation applied or not?).
- Are services being outsourced to 3rd party providers? (Wealth management, technology, investment platforms).
- How large will the back-office support systems be? (Paraplanning, fund research capability, client review and servicing).
- Has the level of adviser charging been considered?

ii) *Restricted advice:* The alternative to independence is a move to a specialist role that provides clients with a smaller universe of options. This would be a more tailored approach in providing 'best of breed' products, vetted for their suitability to the client's needs. Such restriction may actually become the norm post RDR due to the potential rise in cost of financial advice and indeed the lack of knowledge provided by Government and regulators to the consumer.

Banks may actually also decide to take this route because (and its common belief in the industry) it is likely that the majority of clients will either orphan themselves or move to the banks due to a fall in IFA numbers and a misunderstanding over fee charging. Restricted advice may be a cost effective way for the intermediaries and banks to offer financial services.

Restricted advice would make sense for IFAs that are smaller organisations or who belong to a network that too has decided that restricted status is more cost effective.

Wealth managers face the issue of offering a 'fettered' approach in employing a fund of funds approach and thus need to carefully consider the funds used and offered. These funds will vary through most retail investment products (RIPS) and distributor influenced funds (DIFs) that are effectively unitised client portfolio's and allow bespoke portfolio's to be built in a tax efficient manner.

EU Undertaking for Collective Investments in Transferable Securities Directives.

UCITS III rules now allow funds to mix pooled and direct securities and alternative assets, a fund structure can be used to replicate almost any discretionary portfolio.

UCITS IV rules
Replaces simplified prospectuses with the Key investor information document, which includes a risk and reward indicator.

The issues here relate to remuneration i.e. the RDR principles will ban funds or portfolios offering retrocession payments. Uniformity of fees is imperative, thus it needs to be decided whether it's realistic to continue to package DIFs and offer pooled structures either directly or independently.

Solutions:

One such solution could be for both IFAs and wealth managers to become general practitioners, in a similar model to that used by the health profession. This will ensure clients are offered as comprehensive a service as possible, yet with the ability to refer to 'specialists' as and when needed. Indeed such business models already exist in the industry and successfully service their clients with both direct advice and outsourced service. This allows business to hedge their offering and give the client a one-stop shop to cover all relevant market issues.

i) *Passive model:* An option tied into restricted advice is the move by advisories from an active advice to a passive model. This means a service of investment strategies, such outsourcing to Discretionary Fund Managers (DFMs), or exchange-traded funds (ETFs) and index-tracker funds that track the market indices at a relatively low cost to the clients. Total expense ratios would be reduced to under 0.3 percent per annum for ETFs for example and this may aid return on investment for the clients as per the view on the investment value chain in Chapter 3. (N.b. beware 'broken' intermediation for DFM on platforms which may result in VAT charging). 🐦#RDRBOOK

ii) *Simplified advice:* Although this may actually form part of restricted advice, the recent focus on simplified advice has been seen as a 'panacea' for the majority of intermediaries and wealth managers affected by the RDR.

Such an offering will allow advisories to reach the majority of clients, who in turn may themselves be disenfranchised by the RDR as independent financial advice becomes too expensive.

Simplified advice involves less complex structured products that can be delivered cheaply and quickly to the market and has its roots in 'primary advice'. This idea was floated at the time RDR was in its infancy and also has strong support with industry bodies such as the ABI.

Basic advice is a similar concept, but actually sits in its own regime and outside the Markets in Financial Instruments Directive (MIFID). It is designed to provide cheaper products that offer good value to the consumer with caps on charges and increased product flexibility. Yet it is seldom used within the industry, because it was a change to product design led by the regulator. This tells us that if simplified advice is to take off and plug a huge potential gap in the advisory market then the industry itself must lead the simplified market, not the Government or regulators.

There are some key advantages that encourage simplified advice in the advisory market;

a. Ease of delivery: Through Internet, telephone and face-to-face, simplified advice should be simple to explain and understand.

b. Suitability: This should be self evident to the practicing professional and indeed a fact find will always be necessary, but for those clients needing a vanilla style solution simplified advice may suit.

c. Adviser Charging should be clear and easy to understand: With the banning of 'factoring' (products advancing adviser charges), simplified advice should, in theory, provide a transparent platform for product and fee charging.

iii) *Non-advice: Execution only*

There are rumblings that the EU's PRIPS review will ban execution only services where clients effectively buy products non-advised. At present there are IFAs such as Hargreaves Lansdowne who operate a large proportion of their business through this route. This quite cleverly creates a 'regulatory arbitrage' meaning unwanted regulation is averted with products sold non-advised. Banks used such a regulatory preference system for capital adequacy and credit weighting with the now infamous credit default swaps that involved high risk due to the subprime mortgage market and related defaults.

We must be mindful that with an ever-changing RDR territory absolutely nothing can be taken for granted and this includes the simplified advice proposals. We may see a complete U-turn at some stage with either the industry or regulators deciding that simplified advice lacks the definition or profit margins to be implemented comprehensively and the idea may be dropped altogether. #RDRBOOK

6.2 Strategic Design:

The challenge for any financial advisory company whether it is a bank or an IFA is to structure the front and back office in as efficient a manner as possible to ensure fee charging works for the business (profitability) and the consumer (value). This should be viewed as a reciprocal relationship based on the transparency of the value chain that creates a trust based relationship going forward.

Positioning both front and back office systems together, integrating technology, paraplanning, use of platforms and transitioning with a dual model of commission to fees until 2013 all provide clear examples of RDR implementation strategy. The fee structure itself forms an integral part of this structure and as such will be addressed in detail in the following chapter. However, transparency of fees and careful consideration of the business's running costs needs to be measured to ensure a positive outcome for the client and profitability for the business.

6.3 Product Providers, Wraps and Platforms

With one eye on a potential polarisation of the market, providers need to position themselves with great care with the RDR principles in mind. We have discussed the merits of factory gate pricing for product providers in particular and the emphasis on simplification of product design, features and benefits. This along with potential time bombs such as VAT charging, banning of any rebates and the ring-fencing of client monies for charge payment, all require careful consideration and planning while being executed with the consumer's needs first.

One solution for those product providers attracted to the simplified model is simple products. With behavioural economics in mind, the development of products that provide easy to understand solutions and a fair and clear charging structure would seem a suitable solution to encourage financial capability. However, previous attempts, such as the CAT standards introduced in 1999, failed because they could not compete with non-CAT products.

Under Basel II, International Capital Adequacy Assessment Process (ICAAP) is a new requirement for financial institutions requiring the following assessments

- Pillar I minimum capital requirements;
- The extent of total stockholder funds required to meet a firm's strategy and maintain minimum capital requirements;
- Ensuring that the material risks of the firm are understood by its board and that there is sufficient and appropriate risk management

Four crucial elements in any ICAAP are:

- Assessment (identification and measurement) of the risks a bank is or may be, exposed to;
- Application of mitigation techniques that may help to lower capital requirements;
- Stress-testing techniques; role of the Board of directors and management.

This along with the Basic advice channel set up for stakeholder products and the price caps attached meant that it was both expensive and difficult to compete in the market. There are reasons for hope, as the SMF would argue that CAT was flawed and there seemed to be an appetite for simple products from the consumer.

With Government led initiatives such as Thorenson's recommended Money Guidance website and SMF's product Kite-marking initiative we may begin to see a real opportunity for simple products which offer flexible options, can be easily understood and quickly accessed by the consumer via modern technology and social media.

Wraps and Platforms will no doubt argue they are the future. They provide a simple way for product providers and investors to display and access investment products along with easy to understand reporting systems which use the latest technology. The problem is that there is an argument that they need far more work to have transparent services, charges and indeed how adviser charging will be implemented post 2013. A good example of RDR best practice is implementation of an escrow account to ring-fence client monies and evidence of the use of ICAAP and associated Pillar I (minimums), II (Supervisory) and III (Market discipline) requirements as per Basel II. This will ensure client monies are segregated and protected against liquidity proceedings and keep the monies outside the product boundary.

Ancillary services such as simple legal products - e.g. trusts and wills - could also be a compliment to platforms and their clients after the RDR. Together they could offer a real one-stop solution that clients could believe in and that would make customers more comfortable with a more diversified and tailored service.

Figure 6.1: Operational processes and technology

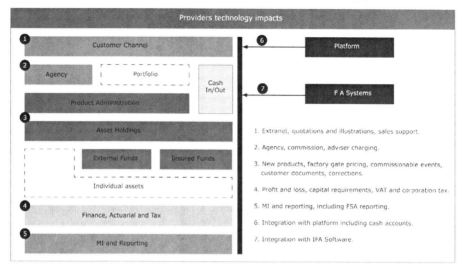

SOURCE: Deliotte; *Responding to the Retail Distribution Review. Adviser charging: Implications of a commission free world.*

6.4 New Business Model Structures and Related Behaviours

As with any business design, changing the internal and external business model needs to be carefully planned and executed. Since the 1950s organisational psychologists and economists have come up with varying theories on change management strategy and the effect of attitudes, beliefs and values on behaviour.

As previously mentioned Kurt Lewin's three step change management theory, the theory of reasoned action or the 6 step behavioural change model may help a business going through the RDR change process to ensure the journey is understood and as smooth as possible for all parties involved. Institutional theory should be examined and understood

Businesses that adapted to market change:

- Levis made spades during gold rush
- Marks & Spencers started with a hand barrow
- Nokia started in wood pulp milling
- Wrigleys started selling soap
- Peugot made salt and pepper grinders

to ensure the business is best structured and positioned for the relevant market.

As we have seen in Chapter 5, academic research into behavioural change continues to intrigue with bestselling novels such as Malcolm Gladwell's 'The Tipping Point'[21] giving guidance on the smallest things and 'influencers' that make business models successful. IFAs, wealth managers, product providers and banks face the challenge under RDR of understanding where their business models need to change (understanding the value chain) and implementing system and behavioural change programmes that ensure sustainable success in 2013 and beyond.

The "mixed business model" one of segmentation of services such as advisers becoming appointed representatives (tied) or multi-tied, or independent dependent on skill, experience, qualifications and staff retention or recruitment of new talent means there is no one way for businesses to re-organise their front and back office functions to benefit from the RDR.

6.5 The Key to a Profitable Business Operation
So in any retail based industry it is crucial for companies to ensure they are adaptable and their business models can change to suit consumer demand. We have a fairly unique situation with the RDR in that financial services is changing completely from a regulatory stance, leaving an industry that must change, but also consumers must change their perception of financial advice and its delivery.

One of the many criticisms of the RDR is that if the premise of the change to fees is to push the bias back to the client, then there has been little done to educate the consumers about how much financial advice will cost. To address this we must firstly ensure that the retail business model is structured to ensure transparency and efficiency of service.

[21] Gladwell M, 2001. *The Tipping Point, The Story of Success,* Penguin Books.

I have devised a number of questions that market participants can include during the implementation phase of business structure re-design: 🐦 #RDRBOOK

1. Does the cost of service delivery relate to client value?
We need to ensure that the business is structured with the consumer in mind at all stages. So the above issues surrounding basic, simplified, restricted and independent advice need to be carefully considered.

2. What are the key issues in relation to service design?
Transparency of fees, costs, risk management, remuneration structures, outsourcing and increased standards of professionalism are all essential factors involved in service design

3. How to evaluate the market opportunity?
Advice levels, the potential polarisation gap, client segmentation, evaluation of the competition all need to be factored in to ensure the market space is identified and then dominated by relevant marketing strategies (see the next chapter).

Figure 6.2: Client Loyalty Ladder

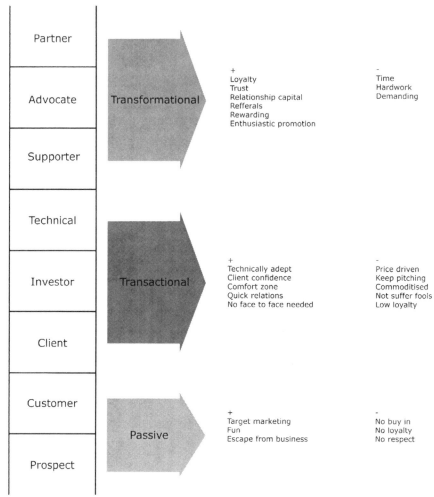

SOURCE: *Engage Partnership Limited.*

As the above diagram shows, client segmentation itself should not mean ditching clients, but evaluation of how services match their needs and then structuring these services appropriately. In accordance with Treating Clients Fairly (TCF) rules, clients' needs must be placed at the forefront of business strategy and the culture of understanding customers' needs should be a critical part of the client segmentation strategy. This means clients may then be segmented in relation to revenue and profit potential, or life stage and of course not forgetting relationship capital (see Chapter 9).

The benefits of this strategy is clients should feel properly serviced, communication is efficient and clear, staff are also clear in their client facing skills and duties and services offered are appropriate for the clients' financial needs.

4. What are the costs of manufacturing fee advice?

The internal and external value chains show us that pre and post fee charging costs cascade down the line which ends up being passed onto the consumer, thus there is the need for high value at all times. Chapter 8 covers the advice fee structure for true and successful fee based charging, yet issues such as advisory time, staff time, office costs, regulatory fees, compliance, software, marketing and client acquisition all take their place in structuring financial advice.

5. What are the costs of manufacturing products?

Factory Gate Pricing (FGP) is normally associated with wholesale products and does apply to the structuring of financial products. A FGP model is already in force and used by some product providers and intermediaries in the market. This is represented by the provider setting a price for their product and the adviser will then factor this into their charging structure which is then past onto the client in the form of cost for advice.

This cost for advice will be paid either by a fee or by inclusion as an additional cost of the product purchased. In both circumstances, the consumer will have to agree how much they are willing to pay for the advice.

In terms of the impact on competition across distribution channels, an increase in competition would require FGPs to become transparent across channels. Multiple FGPs may be offered across different channels, and some providers will offer multiple FGPs even within the adviser distribution channel. However, other providers expect to offer a single FGP to retail advisers.

Whether the FGP becomes a focal point for competition between channels or not will depend on whether product providers and their networks (e.g. banks and larger IFAs) start to compete on FGPs and use them to attract clients. This could mean that FGPs become more transparent and could be used by consumers to compare products and prices within and across distribution channels, although this would require consumers to be proactive in this regard. The Association of British Insurers (ABI) believes FGPs to be the best way forward for RDR fee transparency for all parties in the value chain.

In their RDR report to the FSA, Oxera[22] consider the impact of the RDR on competition within distribution channels and the mechanisms that might lead to higher or lower FGPs in the retail distribution channel. IFAs' incentives to impose pressure on providers to reduce FGPs will be weaker than their current incentive to negotiate high commissions (which result in competitive FGPs at present). This is because, under the current regime higher commissions lead immediately to higher adviser incomes, while under the new regime, a lower FGP will not result directly in revenues to the IFAs. Although they may benefit indirectly from negotiating lower FGPs if they manage to attract more customers and/or increase their sales and profits as a result of these lower FGPs.

Consumers could impose competitive pressure on providers (by shopping around for the best product), but are less able to do so than advisers because they tend to be less well informed. However, if the FGPs become a focal point of competition between advisers, or in the direct sales route, end-customers may reassert this competitive pressure.

6. Has the value of process been considered?
Reducing costs also plays a crucial role, thus natural wastage: duplication of effort and employment of simplified advice could aid

[22] Oxera. 2009. Retail Distribution Review proposals: Impact on market structure and competition. 1-58

a smoother transition. This, along with ensuring consistency along the value chain, also needs to be factored in to ensure teams, departments, management and the organisation's climate and culture are aligned to the RDR vision.

Scalability, including office locations, clients and staff along with a client's perception of value needs consideration. Indeed applying research on the consumers' experiential view of the business can be crucial to future profitability.

7. How to create value?

Value for the client in a fee-based service is created by ensuring the business product and service is consistent, efficient and transparent. This can then build and maintain trust and worth, (relationship capital) a highly desired commodity at present in financial services.

Knowledge and understanding of behavioural economics and the soft skills needed to create client support and confidence can substantially increase the success of the business. So a business plan that knows where the business sits in the marketplace, which particular clients are to be targeted, what exactly it is the business wants to be known for and how to demonstrate its value and worth will succeed.
Areas suggesting high relationship capital:

- Focus on long term relationships and commitments,
- Highlighting client's psychological relations with finance,
- Creating life-long financial plans,
- Building products that are transparent and efficient,
- Bespoke solutions,
- Risk management,
- A balance of behavioural finance with technical knowledge.

A business model that discovers the 'X-Factor' will succeed. As Jim Collins[23] in his business change management book 'Good to Great'

[23] Collins, James, C. 2001. Good to Great. *Williams Collins.*

says businesses that 'discover the single denominator that has the greatest impact on their economics gain piercing insight into how they may most effectively generate sustained and robust cash-flow and profitability'.

As we will see in the next chapter, it's the value the client sees in the financial service rendered, work done and suitability of products that will provide the winning formula under the RDR regulations.

6.6 Summary

The industry is now challenged like never before to employ ingenuity and a collaborative strategy when it comes to structuring the business model. It is crucial to start planning early and incorporate key lessons from institutional theory as described in Chapter 2 and ensure all options are considered when change management is applied:

- Positioning is crucial. As any marketeer will tell you, it's the market participants who grab the key opportunities early to dominate this space that will succeed and thrive. This will apply to banks, IFAs and wealth managers who decide on independent, restricted or simplified advice. Product providers who decide on a simple and/ or a fully transparent product and the platforms or wraps that incorporate full liquidity rules and true adviser charging facilities will also succeed.
- A 'Flip funnel' approach where client needs are considered first and integrated fully into the business model will provide a sure strategy to comply with the RDR principles and engender trust.
- Relationship capital must be a principle incorporated at the heart of the business model.

Case Study 2: A Platform Provider Model

I guess we have been fortunate - RDR has been a bit of a non-event for Nucleus as the key concept behind the business was always transparency. We were inspired by two things:

1. the reality that the life industry had delivered dismal client outcomes for decades;

2. the enlightened IFA pioneers who had worked with Transact to deliver better client outcomes.

In essence we set out to build a business in which the adviser/client relationship was key, where transparency was paramount and in which simplicity was as much of a constant as the regulations would permit. When the RDR came along it didn't feel like a great surprise as the concept had been well-trailed in CP121 - if the industry is ever to build genuine consumer trust and embark on a meaningful, long-term relationship with the UK public it seems obvious that those providing advice must be paid by those receiving that advice. Any other model is hiding the truth and at the very least runs the risk of misleading customers. The RDR therefore is a statement of the obvious, an extrapolation of the work done by the early Transact pioneers and (perhaps overlooking some of the finer detail) something that simply had to happen one day. If the FSA hadn't done it, the market would have. Perhaps it already was.

That said, and although we applaud the principles of the RDR we have still faced challenges - the pace at which IFAs have en masse adopted the new regulations has been frustratingly slow and this has probably impacted our growth. We have also been frustrated by the way in which the regulator has handled some elements of the implementation, and are particularly confused by the work that has been done around banning cash rebates. If rebates are a problem then ban all types, not just the transparent, easy-to-understand ones. If that means that the business models of a few legacy providers are damaged then so be it, there's a greater good to play for here.

All in all we welcome RDR, just as we welcome your work in pulling together this book. Transparency is a 21st century must, and the RDR is the regulatory catalyst that can encourage this philosophy to permeate this most opaque and legacy of industries. Good luck!

David Ferguson CEO

Chapter 7
Marketing Marketing Marketing

"It's not enough that we do our best; sometimes we have to do what's required."
Sir Winston Churchill.

In Chapter 1 we discussed the intended and unintended challenges the RDR makes for retail financial service companies. There is no doubt that one of the biggest challenges is to consolidate and protect market share once the new rules come into force in 2013.

There are many marketing gurus who will be advocating the usual strategies to capitalise on the challenges and opportunities that have arisen since the announcement of the RDR. Yet I argue that the RDR is not usual, it is unprecedented. When before in any industry has there been enforced change across professional standards, a potential attrition and 'brain drain' of market practitioners, quandaries around business models, a distinct lack of consumer knowledge of such change and huge question marks surrounding taxation issues (adviser charge related VAT and product provider income minus expense), and as we will now discuss, marketing strategy?

With all this change, the marketing challenge for financial services organisations is going to be highly complex. I believe the issues are going to be debated in the arena of product development, service delivery and consumer engagement. I shall cover each in detail.

7.1 Product development
It seems that progress is being made by all parties encompassed by this regulatory reform yet product providers have been slower than most to react, maybe playing a waiting game to witness competitors' strategies before announcing their own.

Institutional theory tells us that normative and mimetic isomorphic strategy will play a part in product development along with business models. We are already witnessing the usual market suspects introducing 'RDR friendly' products that will be heavily marketed to the consumer. Those funds, investment/unit trusts and open-ended investment companies (OEICS) already offering institutional priced options have effectively stripped out most of the charges illustrated in the value chain. In theory this should make the funds easier to market and indeed easier to understand by the consumer.

Passive investment products, such as long only investments, index trackers and exchange-traded funds should (in theory) be simple to promote. Along with FGP we may witness a price war with product providers vying for the desired market space.

Figures calculated for the Financial Times by fund research house Lipper[24] show that the average total expense ratio (TER) for an equity fund is 1.68%, compared with 1.18% for a bond fund. Multi-manager funds, which buy other actively managed funds and are often criticised for having a double layer of fees, have a far higher average TER at 2.41%, while money market funds charge just 0.52%. If we go back to Chapter 3 and evaluation of the value chain - taxation, inflation and commissions can dramatically increase these charges so with the bias towards the consumer, product providers need to slash charges to remain competitive and market efficiently.

Passive funds, as they allow lower charges (around 0.3 percent) should decrease the TER so we will see that some fund asset classes are severely challenged by the RDR and some may disappear entirely. A good example is 'With Profits' as they are 'passive' in design but criticised for being opaque.

[24] Lipper, Thomson Reuters. 2009. White Paper. Review of UK fund fees.

7.2 Platforms

Platforms, wraps and supermarkets are looking to take advantage of the RDR and dominate the market. Platforms in particular enable advisers to reduce administration costs and increase revenues by providing a more holistic, high quality and automated service to their customers. By providing this holistic view, advisers manage more of their customers more efficiently. Platforms have changed the approach taken to supporting advice - allowing advisers to be investment led - making the selection of the tax wrapper secondary - and now essentially a commodity.

Market participants such as Nucleus, Axa elevate, Co-Funds, Skandia, Fidelity, Ascentric, Hargreaves Lansdown, Standard Life and 7IM now hold around £150bn funds under management, with an estimate this will rise to over £320bn by 2013[25]: so there is much to play for. Indeed the platform specialist firm, 'The Platforum' has conducted some excellent research and work on comparison of platform charges, costs, features and benefits and stipulate although 77% of IFA business is currently written off-platform, the balance is likely to move in the favour of platforms particularly with larger organisations joining this particular market.

As we have seen, the main issue with platforms is to remain bundled or unbundled where charging is concerned. There is no clear view at present on which strategy will win over the product designers and marketing departments, but as we now live in a world of accountability and transparency surely there is a strong case for platforms to market themselves with unbundled structures?

So with marketing strategies in mind, product providers, platforms and the like will all have to employ transparency and efficiency as marketing strategies, incorporate TER calculations and produce products and platforms that provide real value for their clients.

[25] Datamonitor research store. 2011. UK Wrap Platforms

7.3 Service design

While the retail end of any industry is normally the sharpest and most competitive, financial services takes this to extremes. Therefore, any marketing strategies will need to be incredibly sharp and focused in turn.

If we look at the six stages of financial planning (Figure 7.1) we can see how a service design such as this can be used as a template for a marketing strategy to ensure consumers are well engaged.

Figure 7.1: Creating a service charter

Service	Benefits	Adviser Cost per hour	Admin Cost per hour
Stage One AGREEING OBJECTIVES	We will carry out an initial interview to determine your financial objectives and assess whether our services will be of benefit to you.		
Stage Two DATA GATHERING	We will carry out an in-depth interview to assess your current situation, analyse it against your objectives and identify any gaps.		
Stage Three RESEARCH	We will obtain full information on your existing investments and carry out comprehensive research into your potential options.		
Stage Four RECOMMENDATION	We will recommend the best plan of action to achieve your financial objectives.		
Stage Five IMPLEMENTATION	We will liaise with any selected third parties or product providers to ensure your new plan is set up and run efficiently.		
Stage Six ON GOING REVIEWS	We will continue to monitor your investments to ensure they remain on track to achieve our agreed objectives, and recommend action where required.		

SOURCE: *Royal London 360 Ltd.*

An example of this is customer charters, which are rapidly becoming one of the most popular ways to engage the consumer in the retail sector and it can be seen as a marketing strategy that works. By explicitly defining a business service structure, the business immediately provides clarity and value to the client by explaining what the service is, what the benefits are, who is going to do it and what the cost will be. Without this how do we know that the client can afford the service on offer or indeed that the service is profitable?

Product providers are now marketing 'toolkits' on their websites for use by intermediaries to access information and technology to aid client engagement. I would argue this is the wrong way round. A 'flip funnel' approach needs to be taken to place existing clients first instead of putting all of the emphasis on client acquisition. Providers should be concentrating on those consumers who have already bought a product or a service and thus are already clients of the business. Doing this adds a huge amount of value and garners not only loyalty and trust but also referrals to new clients.

7.4 Consumer engagement

Consumer engagement is a marketing strategy that has already been explored in this book, which if employed intelligently and comprehensively will ensure a business is well placed in the RDR era.

If we go back to the main thrust of the RDR, which was placing client interest at the heart of the change, then a clear understanding of behavioural economics and finance is necessary in ensuring a successful marketing strategy.

As with any business plan, it's

RDR 'Barriers'
- Choice of advice type
- Competition
- Access to markets
- Adviser charging
- Skill shortage
- Limited time for training and development in RDR ready skills
- Costs associated with business model

important to understand the barriers that may stand in the way of retail financial service companies moving through the RDR implementation phase.

A way of overcoming such 'barriers' is a marketing strategy that engages behavioural change policy within the company and attempts to influence consumer buying behaviour in a positive, non-tacit way.

This will mean ensuring that market participants have their skill sets and strategies aligned to the RDR objectives. Government and regulators need to encourage such behaviour by promoting the recruitment of the required right skill set, guidance on product design and education incentives for both market participants and the consumer.

Before we present such strategies, I think it important to review the marketing issues that surround what some psychologists see as the most important issue where financial education is concerned, that of generation Y.

7.5 Generation Y

The next generation has always been seen by marketeers as the most crucial to get 'on side' with the business brand. It has been no different in retail financial services. When I was in my teens, the local bank manager was seen as a stoic and serious figure, someone to look up to and respect and who was generally older and considered wise. I can vouch for this, as my father was a career bank manager!

Such stereotyping has been changed somewhat in recent years with advertisements making banking 'trendy' with onsite branches at university campuses, open office designs of the branch and younger staff with more fashionable uniforms. Indeed we now see with the introduction of social media, a completely new form of marketing strategy that may well revolutionise how we purchase financial services. Imagine a facebook banking facility or a twitter correspondence account dedicated for purchasing life cover... We already see website design evolving to make investing, banking and insurance purchase choices easier. As education of financial awareness in the UK becomes a priority for Government at school level, we are beginning to witness a financial education revolution much needed in a debt-ridden consumer spending driven society.

As I have sat at home writing this book and idly left the television on in the background, I have noticed so many credit and loan advertisements offering quick cash at ridiculous APR (the last one was 1742%!). With such advertising and marketing allowed and little understanding by the consumer of the terms and conditions and their own psychological contract with such, it is no wonder that the UK has the largest debt per head in the EU.[26]

It is my belief that the education of generation Y (and Z) will be greatly helped by careful and intelligently crafted marketing.

So how can this be achieved? Firstly, it's important to take a look at the psychological make-up of the next generation to best understand what motivates them and will aid them make better financial decisions through target marketing.

DECODE's Dilemma
- Gen Y give financial services the benefit of the doubt
- Gen Y feel they have had the 'rug pulled' due to the credit crunch

In a recent interview I conducted with research consultancy DECODE's UK CEO Robert Barnard, I started with what motivates generation Y with their financial affairs. #RDRBOOK

Robert's work extends to uncovering the issues surrounding generation Y's needs and demands in the near future and how best industry may engage them. They want conservative investment strategies and

---

[26] *Currently UK public sector net debt is £867.2 billion. (or 57.6% of National GDP – note this excludes financial sector intervention*

have (as I did at their age) a certain reverence for those working in the UK financial sector. Despite the recent post credit crunch 'banker bashing', there still is an implicit trust from the next generation in financial services. This maybe because they do not have much money to lose, thus any loss would be very hard felt, Additionally, every generation initially feels the previous one understands the complex globalised world. Financial services marketing compounds this with heuristic messaging, i.e. confirming the industry's heightened position through stereotyping and encouraging implicit belief in the system.

This is evidenced in advertisements of people within financial services with austere dress codes, women's position in business being masculine orientated, and the 'knowledge is power' presumption applied. However, generation Y is becoming more savvy to such marketing strategy and is increasingly demanding services tailored to its needs.

DECODE promotes the engagement of the younger generation within the financial services industry by structuring corporate development programmes that aid the co-creation of brand product and messaging. This ensures the industry does not create its product and brand building in isolation, but instead involves generation Y in a positive way.

This is one great example of how a marketing strategy can actually be co-built to allow better information, education and product to be marketed to the up and coming consumer.

7.6 Strategy and Implementation #RDRBOOK
With future generations needs in mind there are several ways marketing can be used to help behavioural economics and choice of financial strategy:

   1. Making it easy
Remember the work published so far on behavioural economics

finds that people do not necessary act in rational ways and this is sometimes (more often than not) taken advantage of by industry. This involves making desirable behaviour easier and cheaper and undesirable behaviour more expensive and difficult. However information and cost on their own are not enough, facilitation of the right 'conditions' is also important. Malcolm Gladwell shows this in his book 'The Tipping Point' where he uses a number of examples where product placement creates certain conditions that enabled individuals to find easy access to the product being marketed and understand its features and benefits.

The book 'Nudge' discusses the pros and cons of choice editing and the 'tailoring' of products offered into the market. Indeed when I joined the financial services industry back in 1990 as a salesman, I was told to market and sell a green, red and blue product, no more, no less. If too much choice is given then clients may experience the 'buridan's ass' syndrome of too much choice leading to little or no action. (Also to avoid my sales technique becoming over-elaborate!).

Such choice editing allows Government, regulators and product providers to play a pivotal role in encouraging positive outcomes for consumers buying financial products and engaging in financial planning.

Default options on pensions are a good example of a keep it simple policy working. Another is ensuring people are given options to sign up for medical cover, but with the proviso they can drop out later (they generally don't). These two show that a keep it simple nudge policy does work and gives the market direction on how to engage a perceptibly lassez-faire society.

2. Making it normal
"Keeping up with the Jones'" is a common occurrence in society, we seem pre-occupied with ensuring we are at the very least on a par with our contemporaries whether inside or outside work. Such

social and cultural behaviour is an opportunity for financial services. It needs to find a way use marketing to make financial behaviour a norm in society, i.e. making it normal to question, probe, self educate on our options when it comes to financial matters.

There are many ways this can be accomplished, by seminar work, choice advertisement, writing articles or books or simply encouraging transparency of financial information within society. The Government's 'Big Society' idea of giving doctors' surgeries full control of their budgets is an example of this. In this proposed model, surgeries are viewed as a business in their own right and need to be managed accordingly, creating (in theory) healthy competition in this particular market, which over time will become the norm.

The name Big Society is meant to encourage individuals to believe they are part of something bigger and better: Its aim is that working as groups can begin a 'norming' momentum to change habits for the good. The Big Society bank has been established with £200 million of government incentives to provide support for local social entrepreneurial business that benefit both business and society at the same time. This style of community based social marketing is a good example of incorporating psychological insights into marketing and focusing on the importance of community engagement and social norms have on changing behaviour. Indeed what we are witnessing is a return to a desire for a bigger private enterprise sector rather than a public sector in society that will mean self-sufficient social enterprise becoming the norm.

Having lived in Hong Kong for 10 years I can vouch for this in a way, with low tax rates at 15 percent and private enterprise encouraged. It is the expected norm that business is self sustainable and supports the state, not the other way around.

What this is all about is essentially making a strong sense of community the norm in the UK: that we're 'all in it together' and with community role models taking the lead. Generation X and Y will have to handle the debt burden left to them by the baby boomer generation, but with a strong sense of togetherness as the norm, this can be met and handled.

3. Making it personal

We discussed this area when drilling down the client ladder of a financial services organisation. Never before has knowing your client been more important than in the run up to and the implementation of the RDR. With client segmentation brings the need to personalise your service by marketing to your clients' specific needs.

The creation of bespoke products and services is already happening in the run up to the RDR and combined with simplified advice options, we are beginning to see insurance groups and some intermediaries aligning product and services to this potential mass market. Such segmentation allows identification of consumers with similar needs and habits and makes it easier to analyse their characteristics and behaviours. Financial organisations are starting to allocate resources to such marketing activity or using this information to decide that a certain market sector is no longer part of their business strategy. Barclays Capital's removal of more than 1000 in-branch financial advisers and its employment of investment platforms indicates their intention to go with the high net worth clients and market directly through technology to the mass market. (N.b. HSBC and Co-operative have also culled their financial adviser numbers dramatically).

A lot has been made in recent years of lifestyle financial planning where advisers set out to manage clients' objectives with relationship capital rather than just product knowledge and technical support. Such planning relies heavily on the clients having set objectives, but behavioural economics shows that some clients, (even HNW), do not specifically have objectives in mind. So care needs to be taken with such a strategy.

Segmentation itself involves internal and external factors, such as costs and opportunities associated with behavioural change of the consumer and the organisation. Therefore where marketing is concerned stories, mythical journeys, painting pictures of the future and tools such as cashflow modelling can and are used to lead clients down the path of financial education and planning. Such tailored communication gives the organisation some power and influence but should also be marketed to empower the consumer, so they become more self aware and educated about the financial implications of their current and future actions.

What this then allows is a meaningful relationship to be built with the client and the organisations so trust can be built and maintained. Through tailored products, messages and client selection financial services may generate relationship capital that becomes an implicit and natural strategy for the business and creates a culture of reciprocal relations, a win-win mentality.

Social media is now surely the way forward for product and brand marketing. Never before has it been easier to use technology to reach so many and with a tailored approach of sharing information rather than marketing the benefits through telling, we see a personal approach at play, one that is hard to ignore and welcomes clients' interaction with business activities.

7.7 Summary

When pulling marketing strategies together it is so important to begin with a clear understanding of the consumers' needs, wants and beliefs. By incorporating all the above i.e. a multiple approach to marketing and basing this strongly on behavioural economics financial services can begin to rebuild trust in society.

- A multiple approach will mean that the consumer ends up with a clear understanding of financial services and its associated costs and ensure that Which? magazine's concerns regarding a complete ignorance of the costs of fee based advice charging are overcome.

- Marketing though multiple strategies incorporating transparency of the value chain, education of the consumers' psychological contract with their finances, a 'flip funnel' approach and the use of social media will help generations Y & Z find a way to an improved and sustainable relationship with their finances.
- Simplicity, ease of information and meaning: 3 strategies that work and add value.
- Specific use of social media can personalise the business strategy and inform and educate clients at the same time.

Chapter 8

Fee Based Financial Planning in Action

"The RDR aims to put the customer in charge by providing them with vital information about the cost and nature of the advice they are receiving".
FSA

We know there is a debate around the fact that the consumer is not currently aware what the RDR is all about and indeed what effect it will have on them when it is in place. The conundrum the financial services fraternity finds itself in is the very thing that has kept them in business is now being abolished. How can business survive?

Financial services is not like other professions that charge fees such as lawyers and accountants. These professions are generally seen as a last resort, but one that is necessary and so clients can be attracted easily. IFAs at the moment do not provide a service that the public generally sees as necessary. Attracting clients has always been hard, but now fees are being charged on top to increase the challenge.

In this chapter I will discuss the main issues that surround fee based financial planning, incorporating misconceptions and untruths where adviser charging, product design and yes the regulators are concerned.

The RDR introduces a concept called Customer Agreed Remuneration (CAR), which is the alternative to commission and is aimed at removing the perceived stigma associated with the commission system. Yet such a wide sweeping change brings its own challenges or unintended consequences, some of which have been raised by the industry but that still remain unclear and unanswered.

8.1 Commission

Commission based remuneration is generated by upfront payment of a client's investment into a particular product. The products structure then usually holds the client within the investment for a number of years in order to deduct charges that pay for the product costs and the commission paid to the advisory. The problem that has surrounded such an arrangement is the fact that they can be opaque and also costly, meaning the client is not fully aware of the affect of this on their individual holdings.

To better understand this take the value chain example provided in Chapter 1 by Maquarie bank (below)

Figure 8.1: Investment Value Chain

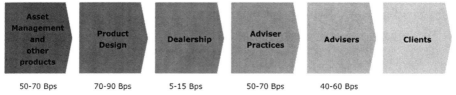

Asset Management and other products	Product Design	Dealership	Adviser Practices	Advisers	Clients
50-70 Bps	70-90 Bps	5-15 Bps	50-70 Bps	40-60 Bps	

Total (Approx) 250Bps + Inflation

SOURCE: *Macquarie Financial Services Group.*

This simple evaluation of an investment value chain shows the TER passed onto the client is 2.5 percent (250 Bps), which also does not include any personal taxation or inflation. This means that with inflation at four percent, the adviser or fund manager needs to be performing in excess of seven or eight percent per annum to give the client a return on their monies. How many investment strategies do we know that give this year in year out?

The commission stated above, that might be taken annually by the adviser, fund platform provider or investment management company, is called renewal commission trail. If we remember back to the behavioural economic issues surrounding 'hyperbolic discounting' and maintaining the status quo, the consumer generally only focuses on the short term and suffers from procrastination, which can be seen as falling right into the hands of the above commission driven remuneration value chain structure.

Commission to fees:

"This investment will cost you £7000 spread over the next eight years Mr Client" to " To place my recommendations to you into effect Mr Client this will cost you £7000, please make your cheque payable to .....

If we add to the equation the issue of bundling of charges that wraps, platforms and products employ, then we can see that the whole system is confusing and opaque.

In favour of commission is the argument that plenty of free advice is given by the adviser or business to secure the client's buy-in and if charged sensibly (and with full disclosure) the client should be aware and comfortable with such a structure. Indeed the selling point when I was an adviser was that limited up front commission with an annual trail commission built in would give the client great value as I would have to do a good job on his investments in order to retain the annual commissions. This also relates to building value in a firm's business. i.e. a reasonable reciprocal trade off one could argue.

It is this conception of 'free advice' that Which? and the ABI are concerned about. Clients may well struggle with the move from payment of commission within the investment structure to the physical handing over of fees.

There are still huge discrepancies where the RDR communication is concerned on commission payments.

- The RDR does not apply to non-advice and in that case a client could in theory still pay a commission, so there is a strong clamour for execution only business to be upheld in the new system
- Trail commission arranged pre 2013 may still remain in force (for a period), yet RDR rules technically ban all trail 2013 onwards

- Savvy orphaned clients (e.g. sacked their IFA) will remain unengaged due to fear of trail fees being challenged. Will this mean that all or part of the commission can continue to be claimed by the platform, wrap or provider?
- Can orphaned clients receive advice directly from the product providers? (N.b. simplified advice maybe the answer)
- Product providers are taxed on income minus expense, this system may well now be defunct as commission comes from expense and in theory any rebates passed onto the product charges. How will this affect product manufacturing?

The above points along with a commission mindset that the industry seems to be 'suffering' from a top down level (i.e. thinking and communicating in commission terms from regulators downwards - see adjacent Hector Sants quote), means that an abundance of confusion surrounds the removal of this system.

The consultancy papers that the FSA has commissioned are laudable, but can also confuse, particularly the paper on platforms (CP10/29) that is currently being reviewed by the regulator with a follow up paper due out in the 3rd quarter 2011 (see additional resources 5). The discrepancy here is the fact the regulator may take a compromise on

Hector Sants 'commission mindset'?

"Payment could be a fixed charge, it could be based on an hourly rate, reflecting the time taken by the adviser to perform the service, it could be based on a % of the amount invested or through some combination of these methods. Some customers with a lump sum to invest may wish to pay for advice upfront. Others may wish to invest a regular amount each month and so be unable or unwilling to pay for advice at the outset. In such cases there are a number of different charging structures that can be adopted, for example, spreading the payment over a period of time. This might be by means of a regular payment to the adviser, or if the product provider agrees, customers would also be able to ask for their adviser's charges to be paid out of their investments.

FSA submission to the Treasury Select Committee December 2010 bundling and unbundling of charges on platforms, thus a commission style structure may actually pervade into the RDR new world order in 2013. In practice this may be unavoidable as some charging structures will be hard to unbundle, but again the industry itself is suffering from some hyperbolic discounting as in the medium to long term, fee basis once agreed with the client will eventually take control of existing commission style arrangements.

8.2 CAR

The FSA describes the new style remuneration in a manner that evokes the factory gate pricing structure we discussed in Chapter 1. i.e. product manufacturers price the product, excluding charges, to cover costs of remuneration to advisers for their services. It is then up to the advisers and their clients to agree the levels and patterns of remuneration in the context of a discussion of all services being supplied. Additional charges are then added to the product charges to reflect such agreed remuneration.

If we move back to the unintended consequences and business models to be developed by retail advisers, we immediately see a quandary. What about VAT?

VAT as a consumption tax means that this would be billable by the business to their client upon procurement of advice not the purchase of product, thus the industry may see great value in going down the simplified advice route and/or offer a 'split' service to attempt to minimize VAT impact. As discussed in Chapter 1, VAT is a potential Achilles Heel and could inflate the cost of financial advice, so with the ABI and HMRC working hard to clarify the position, the industry awaits with interest how this will play out.

The essence of the RDR where remuneration is concerned is to minimise the influence product providers have on setting the price for an adviser's services and no incentivised payments are allowed as a marketing tool to make the product seem more attractive. Advisers will agree a price for their service with their clients, which can be a fixed rate for specified work, hourly rates, agreed percentage of the investment or a combination of all. Fees for initial services are separate from ongoing services.

The fees are then paid directly by the client or through the product and the product provider would agree to take the charge alongside the investment charge. An example of how fees may be taken is shown below, which also gives an idea of how financial advisories may build value within the business based on the fee model.

Figure 8.2: Building fee value

Year		Recurring Income
Year 1	Start recording your time	
	Analyse result and create service proposition	10%
	Write to existing clients advising of planned changes	
Year 2	Calculate costs per clent and compare to actual income	
	Start billing new clents and existing clients for new services	30%
	Write to unprofitable clients with alternatives	
Year 3	Start billing existing clients	50%

SOURCE: Scottish Provident Ltd.

The below diagram also illustrates an example of how capacity and capability may be built for the financial advisers themselves when 1540 client facing hours are taken into account (205 working days x 7.5 hours a day).

Figure 8.3: Annual fee based earnings

	Financial Planning	Financial Advice	Financial Transaction	Total
% time available per client group	33%	56%	11%	100%
Annual hours split per client group	509	862	169	1540
Hours spent with each client	20	10.75	5.5	
Total No. possible clients	25	80	30	135
Income per client	£4000	£2000	£1000	
Total Income per adviser per year	£100000	£160000	£30000	£290000

SOURCE: *The personal finance society.*

The problem we have with CAR is this can be seen as commission offset, i.e. similar to rebated commission as agreed with a client at point of sale. Indeed with a commission mindset permeating the industry, there is a need to define fees and remuneration once and for all.

If fees are carefully and correctly structured and implemented it will aid the consumer through an understanding of the breakdown of costs and charges. It will also help the business actually build value over the years in a similar fashion to commission earnings, with what is essentially more control given to the client and adviser as well as full cost disclosure. If markets and funds under management collapse, maybe fees will be a welcome offset to balance potential loss in income?

8.3 The Bare Faced Fee  #RDRBOOK

With the above information in mind, and in particular a commission mindset, which permeates the industry, we still have much confusion over how fees are to be handled and collected by the product providers and advisers. Indeed as mentioned some market participants view CAR as commission offset. The fee itself is just that, an agreed transactional payment made by the client for services rendered and thus must be ring-fenced as such. This means that present discussions that surround 'commission style' cross subsidies, for example cancellation of investment product unit allocations, do not apply. As we have seen there is to be no return to the days where products would bundle charges incorporating initial units, allocation rates, policy fees, annual management charges, exit penalties and so forth.

The six different methods for charging fees as identified by JP Morgan's comprehensive paper on adviser charging sheds light on the key areas a business needs to consider when deciding on the most appropriate charging model. Again, as with business model design, the client needs to be placed at the centre of such decisions to ensure an engaged and inclusive process is accomplished.

JP Morgan's Adviser Charging paper:

Charging methods;
1. Time-based
2. Task-based
3. Ad valorem (percentage based)
4. Retainer fees
5. Performance fees
6. Contingency fees

May 2011

As mentioned the much-maligned FSA consultation paper 10/29 on platforms can be seen a good example of how confusion is enhanced by mixed messaging. The regulator's obsession with transparency seems to be compromised by this paper's 'Mexican standoff' over the co-existence of platform bundling and unbundling of charges. Additionally, commission style rebating of charges is banned, yet we have industry discussion surrounding rebating to clients through trading accounts.

8.4 Charges, Fees and Rebates

We need clarity and certainty in the direction the industry is to go with adviser charging. With commission speak all we achieve is confusion and asymmetry of information. If platforms are again taken as an example, we effectively have three current models for charging:

1. Rebates from and charges to fund managers to pay for the platform, which means the clients never see the costs accrued and pay the annual management charge (spread across advisers, investment managers and provider).
2. 'semi-unbundled' approaches that separate the investment, platform and adviser charges with any rebates going to the client not the provider.
3. 'Semi-bundled' approaches that are a mix of points 1 & 2 and try (valiantly) to offer the best of both worlds.

It is imperative that the regulators and industry begin to show clear direction on how adviser charging is to take affect and in particular with rebating if this indeed is to be dispensed with in entirety? An adherence to true fee charging would suggest so.

8.5 Regulatory Direction

We want to avoid the inherent ability of the regulator to 'bayonet the wounded' when it comes to charging. The industry is not (yet) in an environment of self-regulation, so direction is needed on what charging behaviour is not to be tolerated - rather than retrospective punitive action. Unfortunately Hector Sant's remarks are open to interpretation, for example where rebating itself is concerned. If

FSA CP 11/8: Data Collection, Retail Mediated Activities Return – RMAR.

Regulatory supervision of data collection through RMAR will cover AC structures and notification on restricted or independent advice and initial or ongoing advice provided.

this does find a way into the RDR world, then will this be allowed to go through the trading accounts before client accounts, will VAT be chargeable? These questions need answering sooner rather than later if AC is to be transparent and fair. In theory, the transaction needs to not only be agreed by the client but also be paid directly by the client and if a client account is to be used then this needs to be ring fenced (e.g. an escrow account) to provide Chinese walls to protect this system along with incorporating ICAAP rules.

8.6 Platforms and Re-registration

With platforms and costs we also have to take into account the issue of clients who wish to or who are advised to move their investable assets from one platform to another. This process known as re-registration can in theory incur charges, tax liabilities and cause disinvestment - highly undesirable. The good work undertaken by the Tax Incentivised Savings Association (TISA) and the UK platform group made up of key industry participants, has resulted in recommendations on a set of standards to deliver a streamlined platform-to-platform re-registration solution with industry standard messaging system ISO 20022 employed over the Swift network. This means an automated low cost solution and importantly where behavioural economics is concerned, a potential end to client inertia in offering transfer options.

It is also worth noting that in the late 1990s the Australian regulator made a U-turn on rebating when implementing new laws on remuneration. This was in relation to industry fears that while fees could be payable initially, it was far too easy for the clients to 'turn off the tap' and orphan themselves after say two to three years if they wanted.

What all this means is that an efficient, transparent and sensibly costed method can be employed for transferable assets and ongoing advice needs, but the logistics still need to be decided.

8.7 AC and Taxation

The RDR has given the industry an opportunity to reinvent itself. This means a fresh start on positioning client relations, business structure and strategy. However, one of our challenges set out in Chapter 1 that causes huge amount of concern is that of taxation. It is becoming quite evident that VAT, Income Tax (IT), Capital Gains Tax (CGT) and Corporation tax (CT) have not been thought through with the unintended consequence (believe it or not) that the cost of advice could increase. To this extent the ABI, IMA and HMRC are now working hard to explore the complications that have arisen from the RDR's move to fee based advice. Key issues that need answers are:

1. VAT: we are clear on what is 'Vat-able' - intermediation i.e. advice and not, product sale and purchase.[27] The problem is around rebates which apply to platforms and funds: The FSA rules are defined around 'ongoing payments' which may be VAT-able or not.

2. Income tax: No reduction in rebates brings lower annual management charges (AMCs), which should lead to higher net income and fund distributions, which may then lead to higher IT and VAT!

3. Capital Gains Tax (CGT): With unit redemptions paying AC within the product boundary, CGT payment then depends on the threshold is breached.

4. Income minus Expense (I-E); This is the system life companies use for taxation. If AC is not now to be an expense as commission was, then the product providers could suffer increased taxation. Trail commissions at present are offset as an expense this will no doubt change when AC is implemented and indeed was planned under the

[27] Note ruling on Insurance wide Ltd v HMRC 15th May 2009; Judge Evans-Lombe ruled that services (intermediation) tied to product sale were exempt from VAT

2011 budget with a January 2013 introduction. This opens a can of worms particularly where qualifying (tax exempt) products are concerned and chargeable events (e.g. partial encashment) may occur.

8.8 Summary

A clear concise communication needs to be delivered on how adviser charging will not be charged. Confused yet? The industry needs to understand that fee based charging will work as just that, a fee paid by the client. For instance solicitors' professional account rules stipulate that client money must be held in a separate client account, on trust for the client. Funds cannot be transferred to the office account e.g. for paying fees without prior client approval and agreeing the itemised bill before payment. If the RDR objectives of 'professionalisation' are to be enforced then such a charging structure should be employed within financial services.

Taxation is always a difficult and relative topic and it is good to see activity undertaken by the IMA, ABI and HMRC in attempting to resolve the unintended consequences surrounding taxation of product providers, advisories and clients. A clear direction will aid transparency of the RDR directives.

- A clear definition of the relationship between client and organisation needs to be settled and understood well before January 1st 2013.
- Fee charging in practice is a transaction between the client and the firm, not a commission offset and (at present) without rebates attached.
- AC Taxation needs to be tackled head on and given clarity by all parties affected.
- Imagine 'a perfect storm': markets crash, legacy fee trails collapse but client fee collection remains. A suitable trade off?

Case Study 3: Solicitor Fee Model

Solicitors are no different any other industry: we go out and get our clients where we can. Instructions are ultimately a result of personal relationships which are cultivated over time through direct marketing, education (seminars and articles) and brand awareness (sponsoring conferences) and of course, the never-ending lunches.

For those of us who deal with corporate clients, repeat instructions mean that our clients are well known to us, and known to be credit-worthy (if often slow payers). New clients however are generally required to pay money on account before we start to do substantive work on their behalf. In either case, any money which comes in from a client (except for payment of a bill) is held, in accordance with the Solicitors' Accounts Rules, in a separate client account. This money is ring-fenced and cannot be transferred to our office account (even if a bill is long overdue) until the client has agreed the bill. The rules are clear - the money belongs to the client until the client says otherwise.

When we accept a client's instructions, we write to them with our terms and conditions and a client care letter. Those terms and conditions will spell out our charging structure. In general, we charge on time spent and detail hourly rates of the individuals who will be working on the matter. As a matter of good practice, we try to ensure that the work is done at the appropriate level, with simpler matters being handled by a junior (who's charge out rate is less) albeit supervised by a (more expensive) partner. Each hour is broken down into 10 x 6 minutes units and the time is captured on software designed to not only assign the work to the right file, but which allows us to provide a detailed summary of how that time was spent.

This produces a bill narrative which is given to the client so he can see not only how much time was spent, but what was done in that time.

Some clients don't like this fee structure and in the current economic climate, there is increasing pressure to come up with inventive alternative fee arrangements. Sometimes projects are undertaken for a fixed fee, or are broken down into smaller individual stages and prices are agreed for each stage. The challenge is to become increasingly creative and competitive, and yet profitable.

Chapter 9

Hard case for the soft skills

"Be not disturbed at being misunderstood; be disturbed rather at not being understanding."

Chinese proverb

Emotional Intelligence: Hard facts to prove soft skills are essential:

Research on 181 jobs at 121 companies worldwide showed of the three abilities vital for success, two were emotional competencies such as trustworthiness, adaptability and a talent for collaboration.

According to a study of what corporations seek when they hire MBAs, the three most desired capabilities are communication and interpersonal skills and initiative -- all of which are elements of emotional intelligence.

Emotional intelligence matters even in the most surprising places. In computer programming, the top 10% of performers exceeded average performers in producing effective programs by 320%, and the superstars at the 1% level produced an amazing 1,272% more than average. Assessments of these top performers revealed that they were better at such things as teamwork, staying late to finish a project and sharing shortcuts with co-workers. In short, the best performers didn't compete -- they collaborated.

Studies of close to 500 organisations worldwide indicate that people who score highest on EQ measures rise to the top of corporations. Among other things, these "star" employees possess more interpersonal skills and confidence than regular employees who receive less favourable performance reviews.
SOURCE: *Daniel Goleman 1995 "Emotional Intelligence: Why it can matter more than IQ"*

One of the first casualties in a recession is frequently the training and development budget. Focus tends to shift to business survival and bottom-line results are king. RDR is no exception with a current focus on the business and remuneration model, fee structures and the attainment of 'professional standards', i.e. QCF4: qualifications driven by the regulatory carrot and plenty of stick.

9.1 Psychological attributes

In the first chapter we saw that economic behaviour and behavioural finance have little influence in the RDR directives. Yet David de Meza et al in their consumer research paper 69 suggest that it should be otherwise: "people's financial behaviour may primarily depend on their intrinsic psychological attributes rather than information or skills or how they choose to deploy them". The paper also illustrates how financial capability does not align with economically rational behaviour.

This equally applies to the consumer and the financial services employee. It highlights the need for assessment of the psychological aspects of the effect RDR will have on all parties. Assessment of clients' needs, expectations and objectives has never been more important. Wholesale or retail, it is now imperative to understand how to maintain and engage client relations.

9.2 Risk management 🐦 #RDRBOOK

The FSA publishes consultancy papers on this area alone. Their recent guidance consultation paper; "Assessing suitability: establishing the risk a customer is willing and able to take and making a suitable investment selection" needs to be understood in relation to the client's appetite for risk, by overcoming perceived shortfalls in collection of client information, the use of risk profiling and asset allocation tools and a clear description of attitude to investment risk and investment selection.

Behavioural economics cannot be ignored. It may be just as important to assess the capacity of clients to take risks and the consequences of any adverse outcomes, as it is to assess their attitude to risk.

So a focus on the hard and soft facts, ensuring transparency of the firm's advice and investment value chain is clearly communicated and risk assessment is fair and accurate, is now so important to get right. What is essential is a focus on the soft skills that are needed for firms to deliver their services and engage their clients to maintain trust and satisfaction successfully in the run up to and post-RDR.

Soft-skills complement hard-skills and are an important contribution to the success of the organisation. As we have seen business success post-RDR requires a 'transformational style', holistic model to ensure advisers build trust across the sector.

As can be seen from Daniel Goleman's and subsequent researchers' work on emotional intelligence, soft-skills and self awareness in how we react to our situation and others cannot be ignored and are essential ingredients in ensuring that employees and advisers alike have their core skills honed to engender and foster client trust with the move to fee-based planning.

9.3 Better Client Relationships (BCR) 🐦#RDRBOOK

Change, renewal or transformation programmes are critical for ensuring RDR readiness and ensuring the firm is more flexible and adaptive. However, as change initiatives can be stalled or derailed, it is imperative organisations devise their RDR programmes as a solution to and commitment to the required change and RDR development.

Financial Skills Partnership; National Occupational Standards (NOS):

Surprisingly relationships & advice standards are not included in the modules! Engage Partnership Ltd have therefore recommended *'Understanding client Behaviours'* as a supplementary and necessary module.

When used together, hard and soft skills enable business leaders and consultants to analyse their current state, envision and communicate the desired, and identify the most important levers for moving the organisation and its people in the preferred direction.

Soft skill orientated RDR programmes will strengthen the organisation and ensure RDR readiness through individual, team and cultural development.

By incorporating work completed on behavioural economics and social scientists such as Robert Cialdini, David Maister, Kevin Dutton and Richard Thaler and Cass Sunstein and others, a dynamic understanding of the desired client relationship with the firm can be forged. This is focused on the understanding of client behaviours in relation to their psychological contract with their finances and will lead to ensuring sustainable relations are built around the concept of relationship capital and trust which is necessary in the new RDR compliant business environment post January 2013.

9.4 Designing a RDR cultural transition learning and development programme

As and when the soft skill arena is acknowledged and understood, it is important to begin to tailor learning and development programmes to ensure the key area of engendering and maintenance of client relations and trust is incorporated throughout the organisation.

There is no doubt that there will be a demand for a new skill set post RDR. As we have seen in the previous chapter through the 'bare faced fee', adviser relations have most definitely shifted from technical and product knowledge to a required understanding of consumer behavioural economics.

Below I point to a 7 step learning and development programme that may help facilitate such a shift in personnel development, recruitment and training: to ensure the right people are in the right place with the right skill set.

Step 1: From training to learning:
There is a strong need for any RDR soft skill orientated programme to shift from a traditional regulatory led 'school room' content-based intervention approach to desired changes in behaviour to a self-directed work-based process, promoting adaptive capabilities and creating the right cultural work conditions to facilitate such learning.

Such a strategy has both a top-down and bottom-up requirement: building a bridge of learning and development from the government or regulator to staff and consumer. Ideally, a climate of shared experience is created where all parties learn from each other to generate a team ethic based on trust and sharing the same objectives and passions. This could incorporate management responsibility for generating commitment amongst employees and vice versa by empowering employees to take ownership of their own self-development, or the regulator building a learning capability for organisations to benefit. This means any commitment gained by market participants' maybe transferred into productive value for the RDR principles of 'professionalisation' and consumer bias and trust.

This type of learning and development focus would create a sense of purpose across the organisations concerned and give employees the opportunities to act with commitment and gain access to a supportive learning environment. This means a continuous learning cycle is encouraged. There are now a number of independent non-governmental organisations that promote such strategies such as Investors in People and the Financial Skills Partnership (formally the Financial Services Skills Council) along with private consultancies specialising in RDR learning and development.

Step 2: Building learning capabilities:
The need now is surely to recognise the importance of developing the required soft skills. The current emphasis is on building client trust and commitment around a completely alien remuneration strategy: one that if left unchecked will mean clients may orphan themselves from the very organisations and relationship managers who can actually help educate them through the fee paying process and the value this offers.

So learning is taking place whether we wish to encourage it or not. There's plenty of RDR related material on the web, so savvy organisations will already have some type of learning and development programmes on the go. It's now imperative to ensure those programmes are fine tuned to meet clients' needs, not just the needs of the business.

Step 3: Shift the emphasis:
Employees' expectations of a regulatory-led training programme delivered to them by the 'ivory tower' brigade needs to change. The FSA have conducted 'RDR-road shows' where the expectancy was a teaching, not a learning, experience: one that often, was not particularly relevant to the industry professional's day-to-day duties.

Responsibility needs to be engendered whereby organisations self regulate and take ownership for their learning and skill development

Step 4: Coaching as a leadership or management style:
Social science and research around leadership and management styles indicate that a manager's style permeates down through the teams they manage or lead, generating imitative behaviour. In their book 'Emotional Contagion', Elaine Hatfield, John Cacioppo & Richard Rapson[28] argue that mimicry is one of the means of how human beings infect each other through emotions. Salesmen for example are often trained to copy their clients' facial features and emotions in order to fully engage their prospect in the sales process.

This 'mirroring' approach can give the lead to the leaders who manage their employees by an 'outside-in' approach. In other words, leaders maybe able to overcome their subordinates' implicit views of their leadership style, by using techniques to move through set views and expectations of how they can act rather than just offering a tailored leadership solution to such latent views.

Similarly, coaching as a learning and development strategy applies to government and the regulators. They need not be seen as an authority that portrays draconian Dickensian traits, but as a coach that facilitates a team spirit within the industry they regulate.

---

[28] Hatfield, Elaine, Cacioppo, John T, Rapson, Richard L. 1994. Emotional Contagion. Cambride University Press. 1-240.

Step 5: Frameworks for the learner:

Competencies indicate good performance and provide the vehicle to identify individual needs and provide a link between corporate objectives and individual contribution. Competencies should be owned rather than imposed, meaning learning is enjoyable and knowledge is successfully transferred to the trainee.

Step 6: Modular training activities:

Breaking the training down into core areas offers more choice and takes away the pressure of too much information (and that feeling of being a 'rabbit in the headlights'). Everyone has experienced training exercises full of too much or irrelevant material, resulting in boredom and confusion. Modulising the training makes it easier to learn and potentially more pertinent and effective.

Step 7: Reflective practices:

It is always important to build in evaluation of the training programme, but this should also include personal development programmes. During my time in retail financial services, I cannot tell you the amount of time I spent on dull training programmes that had no significant effect on my day to day tasks and performance levels other than a strong motivation to avoid such future 'training'.

Sustainability of learning needs to be encouraged by clear and structured evaluative practices that are reflective in nature and emphasise follow-up and continued support in the work place.

By incorporating the above 7 key considerations within a soft skill learning and development programme, we may begin to see the education process becomes more facilitative than tutorial and more mentoring than managing. If both the regulator and organisations collaborate in such a positive way we may see hard and soft skill training become fun, interactive, and most importantly effective: knowledge is sustained and practiced in the work place.

So what could soft skill programme structure look like? Well the subject is complex enough for a book in its own right. However, for illustrative purposes, I have structured a broad-brush 'RDR relational learning and development' programme below which could be incorporated into any size organisation for all levels of staff

9.5 BCR in action #RDRBOOK

Better Client Relationships; Course description:

Adding to the National Occcupational Standards (NOS) this programme is an introduction to the workings of face-to-face behavioural understanding and communication skills; looking at what affects the client and how participants might take charge of situations. It gives an overview of how important psychology and relationship capital are within financial services, and how relations with clients works at its best, whilst identifying where it can go wrong.

Target Student:

Anyone who wants to find out more about what works with the way you communicate with clients and gain and retain their trust, what gets in the way of you being more effective at understanding client behaviour and communicating clearly to client values and then to develop a range of tools and techniques to help the student be more adept and self-assured.

This is a practical day filled with exercises, case studies and discussion which will give the required understanding, knowledge and skills to handle difficult and tricky situations and give more choice in the way client relations are engage and maintained.

Performance-Based Objectives

By the end of the day, delegates will be able to:
- Explain how behavioural economics work
- Explain how communication works
- Understand the social science behind the required behavioural skills
- Gain active listening and responding skills
- Establish how to see things from other points of view
- Explain the importance of body language
- Develop confidence when dealing with clients
- Demonstrate techniques for persuading and influencing others
- Practice ethics of BCR

Course Content

Behavioural economics and related communication dynamics

This is an introduction to the workings of behavioural economics and face-to-face communication skills. It gives an overview of how understanding client behaviour and judgmental bias works at its best, and identifying where it can go wrong.

Behaviour and Communication and how they work

Understanding the principles of influence: Social proof, Authority, Commitment, Consistency, Reciprocity and Liking. Poor understanding of behaviour and communication is normal for that very reason: it's complex.

Things that affect behaviour and communication skills that count

A focus on behavioural biases and what makes us who we are inside and outside of work and how that impacts on the sense we make of clients and they of us.

How your voice tone affects communication

We have a range of exercises that experiment with the effects of variations of tone. Each person will have the chance to identify their usual style and also consider how their tone affects the way that they may be perceived. From there we will practice ways to change different aspects of our natural style.

How Words Work

We have fun looking at ways to deliberately mix our message and bury its meaning under waffle, padding and jargon. The idea being that if we know how to make our communications worse, we can also see how to make them clearer.

Impact of body language

We demonstrate the power and control the listener has, through body language and attitude. Making ourselves consciously aware of our options means that we can remain on a front foot when it comes to communicating effectively. From looking at the effect of our listening skills, to creating the first and the lasting impression we choose, we will offer a range of tools and techniques that can really make a difference.

Difficult communication situations

Using understanding of behavioural economics and work on influence and persuasion, we cover techniques on understanding how best to deal with clients' biases that may impede financial capability. The idea is that we will draw upon any of the tools and techniques covered over the course of the day.

Working to your behavioural and communication strengths

Using behavioural and thinking tools, we assess individual thinking and behavioural styles. They will then have chance to reflect upon how others see them through the feedback of others.

Persuade others to understand how detrimental irrational behaviour can be

This session will develop participants' aptitude for influencing and persuading others through understanding the universal values of persuasion and influence.

Ethics and Action Planning

The final exercise of the course is for you each to understand the conduct standards needed in engagement with clients and understanding persuasion and influence techniques. Devising a personal plan of action, identifying the personal take-out of the workshop, where participants know they will practice and areas for their development.

Finally we identify what will stop participants putting key learnings into practice and what support you need to help yourself put your newly developed skills into practice.

Although generic in nature this learning and development course maybe adapted for any organisation at any level to address some of the key issues surrounding behavioural change needed for individuals and teams to cope with the new skill set required.

9.6 What will the new skill style look like?

'Know thyself' Socrates

Although all 5 of Goleman's EQ domains are important, 2 are key.

Understanding yourself, your goals, intentions, responses and behaviour and understanding others and their feelings seem obvious. Yet so often do people forget to 'self regulate' emotions and are oblivious their effect on other people. The fallback position is to just go ahead and act in the usual way, irrespective of any previous negative experiences.

Goleman identified the five 'domains' of EQ as:

1. Knowing your emotions.
2. Managing your own emotions.
3. Motivating yourself.
4. Recognising and understanding other people's emotions.
5. Managing relationships, i.e. managing the emotions of others.

Citywire publication 'New Model Adviser' is a good example of how the financial advisory market is moving to recognising the new skill set required by the regulatory change. The shift is from knowing your client, to knowing their hearts and minds and taking them through a journey that matches their buying patterns, wants and needs.

We now have a plethora of sales books and strategies available that propound the new model adviser prototype needed to survive in the new world order, David Maister's et als "Trusted Adviser" is one good example of how focus on the EQ can benefit the client and engender trust and loyalty to the organisation.

"When we wrote about trust in 2000, we stressed that earning trust was not just about the knowledge of tactics or the possession of skills, but required some underlying attitudes or character attributes - for example, a real interest in those you were dealing with, and a sincere desire to help (what we called 'low self-orientation.')" David Maister April 2010

So a knowledge of self and actively being in service, are seen as equally as important as the technical, product knowledge needed to ensure clients are given the opportunity to understand the change ahead and what this means to them.

9.7 The sales experience and the cost myth  #RDRBOOK

A fundamental criticism levied at the regulator in relation to the RDR is that consumer education has not been carefully considered. At time of writing the FSA have only just released consumer advice on their website which is fairly limited in scope and application. So the work commissioned on economic behaviour by the FSA is most definitely a step in the right direction.

"We found a big difference between what customers said was important and what actually drove their behavior. *Customers insisted price and product aspects were the dominant factors* that influenced their opinion of a supplier's performance and, as a result, their purchasing decisions.

Yet when we examined what actually determined how customers rated a vendor's overall performance, *the most important factors were product or service features and the overall sales experience.*

The upside of getting these two elements right is significant: a primary supplier seen as *having a high-performing sales force can boost its share of a customer's business by an average of 8 to15 percentage points.*"

McKinsey Quarterly, May 2010.

Clients' experience of the sales process is just as (and sometimes more) important than the price they are paying for that service. Whatever the industry, consumers want to feel they have been given an excellent service, that their needs (hard and soft) have been met and they will continue to benefit in the future. The management consultancy

McKinsey's research is a good example of the need to understand both behavioural economics and the need for soft skills, as we see customers' subjective overall experience of the vendor's overall performance was not price based but experience based despite their initial protestation that price is key.

So where does this all lead us? Well as Keith Dugdale and David Lambert refer in their book 'Smarter Selling', better buyer relationships hang on the quality of relationship capital between the sales organisation and the consumer. It is now all about relationships that deliver value to both the organisation and the consumer. We now live in a ever more connected and complicated world and with this brings the demand for a high level, highly technical adept and transparent sales process that must be delivered with the consumers' needs uppermost in one's mind.

Neil Rackham is now recognised as one of the world's leading authority on sales. His book 'Spin Selling' was initially panned as too complex and confusing but has gone on to change the way selling is perceived. He illustrates that binary sales methods are now 'not fit for purpose' and soft skills have developed to become more sophisticated since the early days of ABC's (Always Be Closing).

Sales training seems to have come along way since the days of pure product knowledge and client relationships based on transactional engagement. With government and the industry regulators now placing emphasis on financial capability and public policy tempered by behavioural economics, we begin to see the need to place the client at the very centre of the business to client relationship and business model. Consumers are obviously concerned when it comes to fair value, costs, charges and fees, yet it is also the sales experience that is important to them, so it is imperative that financial firms have the right people in the right place with the right skills to ensure experientially consumers are satisfied and trust the process and services offered.

9.8 Summary

There is a fundamental need to include soft skills within any learning and development programme. If the emphasis is on the business services, product or technical skills, the client is not at the centre of the business' interests. Ensuring the business has emotional intelligence and right people in the right place with the right skill set has never been more important.

- Taking time to ensure that staff have the correct communication requirements is crucial during the early implementation of the RDR change process.

- A learning and development programme to aid understanding of how to examine the clients' subjective and objective financial needs will compliment the change management process.

- The sales process and experience is often more important for the clients than costs and product understanding.

Case Study 4: Relationship Capital

That "People do business with people" is a well-known axiom. Ask any person in business for the three most important factors driving the success of their business and "relationships" will be on the list. Strange then, that while systems, processes and measures have been devised to track the value of other business assets such as fixed assets, financial assets, people assets, even intellectual assets - no system has emerged to measure and manage relationships.

Ask someone to rate their relationship with a client, customer or prospect and they are likely to say something like: "Good"; "Great"; "OK";"So-So" or "Not so good". Of course these are subjective assessments. One person's view of a good relationship is not necessarily the same as anothers

Goodwill is the nearest that the accountants have come to attaching a value to relationships, but goodwill is a catch-all intangible asset that comprises more than the value of relationships and is open to challenge. Relationship Capital refers specifically to the value of relationships. For an individual, his or her relationship capital would be the value of all their relationships. For an organisation it is the sum of all the relationships of all the people within an organisation. These relationships may be with customers, colleagues, suppliers, partners, ex-employees, or any other person with influence.

In an individual, relationship capital would be good where a salesperson has a strong relationship with a buyer. It would be higher still where other individuals with whom the seller has strong relationships also have strong relationships with the buyer - or with people who influence the buyer.

Graphically this might be represented thus:

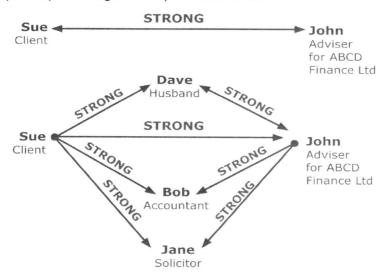

Of course, relationship capital is higher where relationships are with people who have power, influence, or both. Influence is often typically associated with power and we tend to be naturally attracted to power - which often attaches to job titles. Where sometimes mistakes are made is where the influence of someone with a less impressive title is overlooked.

So, factors to consider in calculating relationship capital must include:
1. strength of relationship
2. number of touch points on both sides
3. position (role-based) power and personal influence

There is a problem here though, as noted above. How can we arrive at a more objective view of relationship strength?

Working with Related Vision (www.relatedvision.com) we've devised a system for scoring relationship strength. Answering 10 simple questions relating to the nature of conversations with customers or clients, Related Vision's free on-line meeting assessment tool calculates a relationship score between 0 and 100 and suggests the current relationship type. Partner relationships are the strongest and are represented by scores of 70 or over.

The benefit of the questionnaire and the relationship scores it calculates are that it creates a reference point from which progress can be measured. For organisations, a matrix of relationships and overall relationship strength can be monitored - as shown below - and relationships targeted where action is required.

Relationship Security Summary: Future Media				

Organisation **Future Media**

Customer Profile **High**

Relationship Security **91%**

Position	Power	Influence	Relationships	Overall
NA/Neil De Rossi	High	High	● ○ ●	●
Managing Director & Publisher / Micheal Monaghan	High	High	● ○ ○	○
Executive Director, Marketing / Montana Wallance	High	High	● ○ ○	○
General Manager / Mike Chappell	High	High	○ ○	○
Business Development Manager, NSW Government & Education / Micheal Merry	High	High	○ ○ ●	○
Business Development Manager, NSW Government & Education / Melissa Baker	High	High	○ ○	○
Human Resources Manager / Micheal Lesle	High	High	○ ○ ●	○

Finally, why focus on building relationship capital? As mentioned earlier, we intuitively recognise that business success, and indeed success in life generally, is highly dependent on relationships. Specific business advantages of high relationship capital, deriving from partner relationships with people of power and influence include:

- A better understanding of how to sustain long-term business success.
- Early identification of significant accounts where relationship capital is low and therefore the account may be under threat.
- Lower costs of winning work, since in general the cost of retaining customers is far lower than the cost of acquisition.
- More profitable work because customers want to work with people they trust and so are prepared to focus less on price.
- Better matching of people to people e.g. matching sales reps to buyers on the basis of those best able to relate effectively. The better the relationship the more likely you have an environment in which clients/customers will buy from you.
- More word of mouth promotion and referrals.
- Lowering the likelihood of clients/customers switching to competitors. This makes it more difficult for competitors to enter the market.
- Happier customers leading to happier employees; improving staff retention and reducing hiring and training costs.

The advantages are significant and highlight that relationships are a key business asset, too long neglected by management science. Those individuals and organisations that manage their relationship capital will have a significant competitive advantage in the developing knowledge economy.

David Lambert IOWEU

Chapter 10

Technology, Technology, Technology

"Any sufficiently advanced technology is indistinguishable from magic".
Arthur C Clarke

The retail financial service industry has come a long way since the days of reliance on manually balancing the day's trading, money transfers by telex and the door-to-door insurance salesman. Information technology has not only created new, efficient systems for trading, managing finances and selling financial services, but also new industries and products in its own right.

We cannot now imagine a business world without technological involvement. Moreover, in an ever more connected world; any enterprise without a serious understanding and engagement of technology would soon be out of business. As we have seen with UK retail financial services facing huge regulatory upheaval, this challenge has also extended to the design implementation and employment of technology, particularly since the financial crises where we now witness the need for firm boundaries of trading and better risk management techniques to be enforced.

Successful businesses are automating and managing every aspect of their business operations through investment in information technology (IT). In the financial sector, the focus is on financial and business management software to manage efficient communications, processes and risk. Technology then has an integral role to play within retail financial sales and only those forward-thinking organisations that fully utilise their IT resources, will survive and retain customer loyalty.

Given its essential status, it is helpful to understand where we presently are with technological engagement and how we can develop as business changes and technology develops.

10.1 Social Media

Despite the recent financial crises which witnessed the effect of 20 years of casino style investment banking run amok with our fiscal system, retail financial services is generally viewed as a conservative establishment. This attitude can certainly describe the industry's employment of technology.

We have witnessed a revolution in social media over the past 5 years with the introduction of Skype, facebook, twitter, linked-in, slide share, bright talk, you tube and many more technological based media outlets all of which offer an online information sharing resource that attracts potential customers for business.

Figure 10.1: Global online population

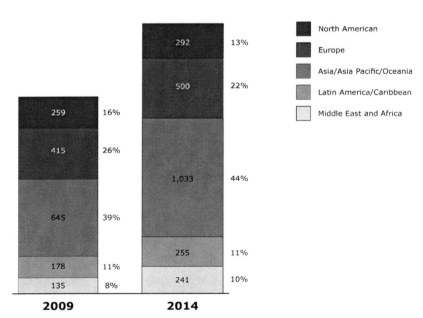

Global online population by region
(millions)

SOURCE: *Forrester Research World Online Population Forecast 2010 to 2014 (Global)*

The digital publishing and training group Econsultancy has published some excellent material and data surrounding the social media phenomenon, illustrating that worldwide users now spend around 4.6 hours per week using social media, compared to 4.4 hours using email. 48% of these online users are reading content (articles, blogs, websites) and 49% are reading and writing emails.

So with such a raft of activity surrounding social media it is no wonder that business is beginning to recognise the need to engage social media and overcome any associated fears in adopting this technology to communicate with potential clients.

Twitter claims to have 190 million users with 65 million tweets a day; Facebook reaches 60 million globally with 30 billion pieces of content. Indeed it is said that, in terms of population, if Facebook was a country, it would be the fifth largest country in the world.

With such a raft of activity

The benefits of customer engagement strategies

Investment in customer engagement seems to be paying off for companies, with almost three-quarters of client-side respondents (74%) saying that their engagement strategy has been either "very successful" (9%) or "quite successful" (65%).

Almost half (48%) of internet marketers believe their company's presence on social networks has resulted in a tangible and measurable improvement to customer engagement. More than half of client-side respondents (58%) say they anticipate their investment in social networks for customer engagement to increase this year, and significantly more companies than last year say they plan more spending on user-generated content (up 13%), and on-site branded communities/forums (up 9%).

Use of social media for customer service

Companies are really seeing the benefits of social media as a customer service channel which allows companies to handle complaints, questions and deliver real-time information.

More than half of the companies surveyed (51%) are now using social networks as a way of improving customer support, 15% more than in last year's survey. Companies are also planning further investment in social channels, with 54% of company respondents and 69% of agency respondents saying they (or their clients) were planning further investment in social media as a customer service channel.

Accenture: Engaging social media
February 2011

surrounding social media it is no wonder that business is beginning to recognise the need to overcome its fears and engage social media in order to communicate with potential clients. In the circumstances, the trend for business to focus on e-commerce, search engine marketing, email marketing, Internet advertising, mobile device applications to spread their messages and services, is hardly surprising.

Social media means big business opportunities. As we have already seen from Chapter 7 there is a need to understand the hearts and minds of generations Y and Z in order for business to survive. Social media is one way to engage with these generations. It brings with it, however, a responsibility to adopt a responsible strategy when utilising social media as a marketing and sales medium.

So what are businesses doing and what could they do better? Professor Merlin Stone, The Customer Framework and the Foss initiatives are all conducting some excellent research on the need for technological application within financial services. They primarily focus on the use of customer management frameworks and technological advanced communication channels to aid the dissemination of financial service information, options and purchase. Preliminary results indicate that at present, banks, IFA's and wealth management companies still have a long way to go to offer a comprehensive, user-friendly IT based service.

10.2 The Cloud

🐦 #RDRBOOK

Technology Blog

"My pet dog can live on a cloud, but my bank cannot - discuss"
John Cant

The fundamental problem is that financial services organisations are systemically conservative when it comes to new technology. This is probably partly attributable to the fact that the use of technology within financial services is risk driven, i.e. implementing and managing the regulatory controls and business compliance systems that are seen as essential to business practice.

John Cant's humorous fictitional essay question opens a healthy debate on the future of technology and financial services. Industry commentators tell us we are apparently now living in the age of cloud computing: where large amounts of data may be stored externally from the computer and accessed from anywhere giving more flexibility and freedom.

Drop-box is a good example of this. Once installed, files maybe created and password protected but accessed through any computer. This form of IT (if held securely) is surely needed in the modern world where financial services is concerned? DECODE's view of generation Y becoming a more 'virtual' worker than ever before, with offices based wherever individuals are able to power up their computer means this flexible approach is needed in any business hoping to thrive in the 21st century. Security remains a concern, but it is fully expected that these teething problems will be rectified as the Cloud providers become more experienced both in terms of the technology and the corporate marketplace.

In addition, there are vastly experienced industry professionals dedicated to providing and improving Internet security, providing the necessary safety that allows financial organisations to at least consider the opportunity that such IT brings. Mike Harris is the founder of three iconic brands: the first telephone banking service First Direct bank, Prudential's online banking service EGG and telecommunications pioneer Mercury 1:1. His latest venture, Garlik, is an internet security company which gives consumers full control over how and where their data appears online and provides products to protect this information.

Technology start ups like Cogent (which offers remuneration management) and Kurtosys (which is involved in client reporting) are now being employed by banks in particular and as social media is now ensuring the next generation will be more savvy to financial products and services than any previous generation, this then leads to a challenging and highly competitive environment for service providers to structure their products in a transparent and efficient way, and communicate their value chains clearly and concisely.

FNZ's emergence as a leading technology and investment administrator is a tell tale sign of the importance now placed in designing the right technological support for the industry. FNZ powers wealth management platforms and currently administers some £16 billion of assets on behalf of over 300,000 end-customers and are involved in designing some state-of-the-art transparent software solutions.

10.3 The 'black box' treatment

Depending on your stance, IT is viewed as a vehicle for communicative distortion, a tool for labour control, a learning and development tool or a production system for enhancing efficiency and adaptability. We see all sorts of computer mediated communication (CMC) methods such as call centers, video conferencing and advertising, being utilised by organisations some of which have been shown to be effective some not so. In some cases technology enhances communication and in others, a face-to-face route may be preferable. It is not the technology per se, but how it is deployed, that decides whether or not IT is fundamentally a "black box".

It really depends on the industry and organisational culture in how IT and CMC is deployed: some feel it enhances communication and other prefer a face-to-face route. Yet there is no avoiding the fact that the next generation has become dependant on IT, social media and CMC. With the RDR's emphasis on consumer needs, such a resource cannot be ignored and must be actively and effectively engaged by the industry.

At this point lets take a look at how IT is deployed within retail financial services to see if indeed a difference is being made to services offered and consumer confidence.

10.4 Cashflow modelling

With the emergence of lifestyle financial planning and reliance on meeting set client objectives, we have seen a number of CMC based technology products developed to map out cashflow analysis incorporating real life critical events such as marriage, family planning, school fees, and retirement. Where these type of tools add value is giving a tangible value to such financial planning objectives. The focus is on how client's savings and income levels will adapt to such life events and what trade-off's need to be made to ensure such objectives are met.

Providers such as Voyant, Prestwood, and Touchstone all provide such tools and we are seeing new developments all the time as the market evolves.

10.5 Asset allocation

Investment decisions made by wealth managers or para-planners have huge consequences, so much so that delivering a strategic asset allocation to match the client's lifestyle objectives and risk appetite is paramount when financial planning. It is now normally accepted 'the modern portfolio theory principles' should be followed when structuring the asset allocation.

Harry Markowitz and Modern Portfolio Theory:

- Modern Portfolio Theory proposed that investors use diversification to optimise their portfolios.
- The theory assumes that investors are risk-averse, meaning that given two assets that offer the same expected return, they will prefer the one that is less risky.
- An investor will therefore only take on increased risk if compensated by higher expected returns.
- An investor who wants higher returns must accept more risk. The exact trade off will differ based on the individual's attitude to risk.
- The implication is that an investor will not invest in a portfolio if a

second portfolio exists which has better expected returns for the same level of risk.

Technology can help enormously here with fund profiling, asset weighting and risk assessment tools that will ensure the client's ongoing and ever-changing needs will be met and tightly monitored.

10.6 Risk profiling
Figure 10.2: The efficiency frontier

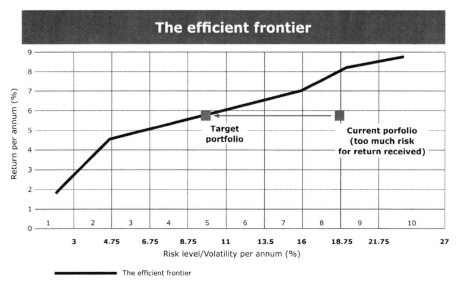

SOURCE: *Distribution Technology Ltd.*

The above chart illustrates the relationship between the return and risk of a portfolio. The portfolio that remains on the curve known as the efficiency frontier provides the best potential level of return for the risk level it is exposed to. So we can see the higher the appetite for risk, the better the return maybe. What modern portfolio theory exposes is the need for diversification. Some companies (like Distribution Technology) now enable financial planners to factor this theory into their systems to give key data when selecting assets for investment portfolios.

The FSA paper on risk profiling makes it clear that a pre-requisite for advisories post RDR is to understand and manage the risk appetite of their clients. This builds on the behavioural economic work that discusses consumers' tolerance and appetite for risk and association potential for loss.

DECODE believes that the next generation are conservative in their investment needs and feel that the current financial crises has pulled the rug from under their feet. Accordingly risk management and associated psychological fears this may inhibit, need to be addressed by the industry. With this in mind there are now a number of tools available that measure and manage the risks associated with investment funds and services. Finametrica who have recently integrated services with UK based Voyant, offer a comprehensive scientific assessment tool for personal financial risk tolerance. Capita Financial Software offer a set of tools to give advisories comprehensive data on 85,000 funds and 124 wrappers and platform provider choice and engage partnership's efficiency and transparency index (eTpI ™) focuses on business process risk management of the value

FSA CP 06/09 Organisational Systems and Controls

The MiFID and CRD requirements on governance, internal controls and organisation are relatively similar. They require, broadly, that a firm has:

- robust governance arrangements;
- sound administrative and decision-making procedures;
- an organisational structure which clearly, consistently and in a documented manner specifies reporting lines and allocates functions and responsibilities;
- adequate internal control mechanisms;
- effective internal reporting and communication of information; and
- adequate safeguards for the security, integrity and confidentiality of information and for the firm's information processing.

chain processes and streamlining for RDR compliance. This along with Engage's 'Viability' activity based costing management software means the industry now has some cutting edge technology available to manage RDR demands.

10.7 Outsourced Support Services

As described in Chapter 6, with intermediaries moving towards either an independent or restricted advice model there maybe the need to outsource services and this will include technology support. The FSA's consultancy paper 06/09 covers the main issues from a regulatory stance regarding the governance and controls required in financial services enterprises. Organisations such as Three sixty, Simply Biz, Paradigm and Sesame Bankhall offer a compliance and business support network model to allow advisers to concentrate on client facing tasks.

The increased emphasis on professionalism can place real strain on existing business models. By outsourcing compliance, training, and business processing requirements, financial consultancies can focus on streamlining their business models to ensure compliance with RDR objectives but also ensuring profitability for the business and a return on investment for the clients.

10.8 Diagnostics

As we have seen from the chapters focusing on behavioural economics and the soft skills needed to ensure the engagement and maintenance of client relations, there is a strong need for organisations to have the right people in the right place with the right skill set and for consumers to become more self aware. Independent consultancies have taken notice of the RDR challenges, and now offer bespoke services to aid financial service organisations with their needs surrounding staff EQ development and awareness. Many administer diagnostic tools designed to highlight the current company profile against the desired behavioural styles and skills needed to ensure that the change management programmes are effectively executed and client relations remain intact.

As the old saying goes: individuals are normally hired for their technical knowledge and fired for their personality. Psychometric and diagnostic profiling have mainly been used historically for recruitment purposes, yet there is now a strong case to incorporate a diagnostically based development programme for the purpose of staff self-awareness and personal development through the RDR change management process. This will ensure that the new demands for fee based services will be best met by those organisations who have invested in their staff's skill development and learning.

Tools such as lifestyle inventories, Myers Briggs and Dominance Influence Steadiness Conscientiousness (DISC) which are all based on social science behavioural models, are now being utilised in the market as development tools to provide gap analysis of staffs' strengths and weaknesses and subsequent formation of self-development coaching programmes. Indicators such as Navitas' 'Think Feel Know' (based on thinking styles and appetite for risk) give a good benchmark for how firms may best interact and understand their clients' behaviours and needs, and place the client at the very heart of the relationship capital developed as a result of such technological application.

10.9 Summary
The RDR brings with it a degree of regulatory and market determinism. In other words, there is no escaping the move to consumer bias and professionalisation. This in turn means that technology advancement and related tools need to be embraced and integrated into the business model. If banks, wealth managers and IFA's are to successfully meet the demands of the RDR, and indeed those of the next generation, then technology needs to be used efficiently, effectively and with a good deal of savvy.
- The Industry must 'get over itself' and recognise technology is a 'must have' tool for client engagement.
- Client-centric technology must be encouraged, enabling clients

to take more control over understanding their financial capability and the products and services offered.

- Technology that facilitates a healthy and educational interface for business and the consumer can only be a good thing.

Case Study 5: Adviser Technology

Over the past decade, changes in regulation and the automation of product delivery have driven the advancement of adviser-focused technology in the UK financial services industry. There is now a wide array of software solutions available to intermediaries to help improve efficiency, reduce administrative time and increase new business volumes.

More recently, with the Retail Distributing Review (RDR) approaching and a reemphasised focus on client service; the move to adviser charging and transparency of charges have encouraged advisers to further embrace the opportunities offered by technology in the form of platforms.

Adequate due diligence of the platform market, however, is not a straightforward task and one which requires regular consideration.

FSA guidance? In 2008 the FSA published its guidance factsheet: *'Platforms: using fund supermarkets and wraps'* which outlines nine key areas which advisers should consider about platforms they intend to recommend:

The platform provider;

Terms and conditions of using the platform;

Charges - including actual cost, charging structure and transparency of charges;

Range of funds, tax wrappers and other products available;

Range of asset classes;

Functionality;

Accessibility;

Additional tools; and

Support services

Synaptic Comparator In July 2010, Capita Financial Software (Capita) launched the Synaptic Comparator service; to specifically help advisers fulfil the new RDR requirements, by enabling advisers to compare aspects of platforms and conduct thorough due diligence as outlined by the FSA in Consultation Paper 10/29.

The innovation, developed by Capita and independent consultants The Platforum, addresses the nine points outlined in the FSA's guidance factsheet, including charges, to calculate the total reduction in yield (RIY) and enable the 'overall solution cost' of each option to be analysed.

As at July 2011, Synaptic Comparator includes data for 20 platform charging structures, over 300 tax wrappers and thousands of funds.

But is platform recommendation always the best approach?

The on / off conundrum Unless an adviser firm has a homogenous client bank, the answer to this question is likely to be 'no'. It is for this reason that a new version of Synaptic Comparator (V2.0) is planned for launch in Q4 2011, which will enable advisers to compare both on and off platform, RDR ready, open architecture investments for their clients, to fulfil the FSA's requirement of advisers to: *"continue to consider off-platform investments where applicable"*.

As part of the development, comprehensive analysis of the current landscape was conducted by Capita researchers who found that as at June 2011 only around 50% of products available were RDR ready. It is clear, therefore that the industry has a long way to go before it is ready for the impending changes RDR will bring.

Capita's 'next generation' software solutions have been designed to support advisers and product providers through the proposed changes. While technology can never replace the experience, expertise and knowledge of advisers, it can go some way to assisting them in offering a level of service demanded by clients and expected from the regulator in a post RDR world. Technology can also provide the audit trail that the adviser needs, with the minimum amount of effort, a valuable commodity in today's uncertain times.

William Watling is Product Director at Capita Financial Software

Chapter 11
Putting it all together

"Interdependence is and ought to be as much the ideal of man as self-sufficiency. Man is a social being".
Mohandas Gandhi

The RDR Journey poses challenges and risks to UK financial services organisations across the board. Since the announcement of RDR some 4 years or so ago, we have seen a whole host of disparate views aired through the media: positive, negative and often disparaging.

As I mentioned at the beginning, I am certainly not purporting to offer a panacea of any sorts when it comes to RDR implementation strategies and change management structures. At the very least I hope to prompt a healthy debate in the market place which can engage all participants including consumers in a positive way enabling better communication and understanding of the reasons for change, the issues faced and the opportunities ahead. It is only through practical and transparent expression of our individual experience with the RDR directives and their perceived intended or unintended consequences that we can begin to move through the fog and gain purpose, confidence and unity in our ability to embrace organisational change and build businesses that benefit all our stakeholders.

I certainly see a huge opportunity for government, industry and regulators alike to learn from the past. I'm not just talking about the recent financial crisis, but if Chapter 2's timeline of historic events is studied and taken into consideration then we can surely build relations with market participants that generate constructive ideas and relations based on understanding, ingenuity and trust. We will always have to contend with the darker side of human nature (think DR Dutton's functional psychopaths) and indeed maybe we need this to spur us on at times of threat and angst, but we have choices as the story of the Native American elder goes:

"Inside of me there are two dogs. The black dog is mean and tries to talk me into making the wrong choices. The white dog is good and encourages me to make the right choices. The black dog fights the white dog all day." When asked by a friend which dog wins, the elder reflected for a moment and replied; "The one I feed the most."

So it is with business in any industry, non-more so than financial services, which in the past has been governed by the most base of human emotions, greed and fear. A balance is needed from the regulator down to the SME or one-man IFA, that inspires a willingness to co-operate and operate functionally with shared values at the very heart of change to the RDR principles.

The only way, in my mind, that this can happen is through transparent and open engagement. The rebalancing of available information, demystification of enforced processes and unconditional education of both industry and the consumer in the behavioural economics that govern individual and business interaction, will bring a certain healing to the RDR implementation process, that although deemed necessary, has caused such consternation to many. So with this in mind, I highlight 7 key areas that if invoked correctly bring together many of the issues discussed in this book to lead to a change management strategy that ensures sustainability of business and positive client relations in the brave new RDR world.

11.1 Honesty

Knowing where you are and why you are where you are, has never been more important to understand. In the first chapter I detailed the main challenges as I see it (at time of writing) to be understood, met and overcome if the industry is to avoid continual dysfunction post 2013.

Let me again point out it is not only the financial services firms fault that the industry has been deemed 'lacking'. Again, the timeline of regulatory activity in this country indicates that a lack of understanding, or willingness to understand, the behavioural economics at play amongst all parties is also partly responsible for the current position and seemingly radical RDR directives at play.

If we take time out and reflect on our respective positions and perceptions within the industry, then we may begin to employ 'blunt candor' in our dealings with the challenges that need to be met. In other words, be completely and totally honest with your journey thus far. Are you really comfortable with the change management steps you have taken and will they give you the outcomes required to ensure productivity and client trust post 2013?

Honesty comes from a place of trust and integrity that can mean 'feeling the fear and doing it anyway'. Whatever your role in the financial services industry, being open and honest about your organisation's structure and how it has been affected thus far and engaging constructively with the continued implementation process will allow both a freedom of expression and a new found level of confidence to achieve in the RDR regulatory arena.

The challenges, whether seen or unforeseen, are what they are - challenges. Thus each day the business needs to re-asses the impact they are having on the chosen strategies in place. At the very least, honesty surrounding the unforeseen challenges will open meaningful debate and hopefully workable solutions. One example is the HMRC's recent communication on adviser charging, and the ramifications from a tax perspective of how this will play out post RDR. In their letter to the financial services industry the HMRC stipulated;

"Although the RDR is the responsibility of the FSA, the Government has made clear its support for what it is trying to achieve. Ministers understand that many advisers and the wider industry are keen to develop systems and appropriate business models ahead of the deadline for changes. In light of this HM Treasury and HMRC officials have been working with the FSA and industry bodies to make sure

that we fully understand proposed charging structures and the tax implications arising from these. Following work to date we have identified some areas where further clarity would be helpful for the industry in preparing for the transition. We are exploring the options around updating HMRC's technical guidance. The areas under consideration include:

- *Updates to the HMRC VAT Guidance and Registered Pension Schemes Manual;*
- *Technical Advice on CGT - acquisition costs and "adviser fees"; and*
- *Products written in trust."*

So here we have a classic example of a need for an open and transparent engagement amongst all affected parties where adviser charging is concerned. The need is, to coin a much used management phrase, to tackle the 'elephant in the room' and adviser charging is just one of the many unaddressed obvious truths.

Recognition of these RDR elephants needs to happen quickly and fast. With many organisations claiming RDR compliance despite much work to be done, a good open and honest appraisal of the key challenges is needed. These areas may include:

- The aftermath of the budget change to the I-E taxation system of insurance companies.
- Positioning of regulatory measures against grandfathering of experienced advisers through the qualification requirements.
- Realistic appraisal of the business and operational risks.
- Distribution channels (e.g. independent or restricted) and client support.
- Platform offerings and related price structures: is a full unbundling of costs a realistic option?
- Product development around simple products and simplified advice.
- Strategies surrounding consumer awareness of RDR and financial capability.

This list is endless. Only you know the key areas that may not have been tackled as fundamentally as you would like and must be tackled.

11.2 Understanding

The value chain is the bedrock of any organisation. Knowing and understanding the value of your business means that you will be able to communicate this with confidence and pride to your staff and clients, which in turn will engender trust and loyalty going forward.

By understanding of the value-chain concept, the delivery of products and services to the end customer creates a synchronised set of interactions of local and external value chains which then go on to create, as Michael Porter describes, a "value system". This system includes all stakeholders who have an interest or are touched by the organisation's activities. Capturing this value is priceless and of great interest to business consultants who wish to ensure their clients stay ahead of the competition and are in continuous improvement via efficient and streamlined value chains.

Where the RDR is concerned, we certainly need an understanding of how a RDR successful business will look. Prototypes currently exist in the market place, but remember the guide map analogy? The really pertinent understanding can only come when we arrive at the destination and see how the landscape looks.

How may we begin to understand our true value and potential? Well one method that has a proven success is business process modelling (BPM). This is a holistic management approach focusing on alignment of all the business internal and external value chains promoting transparency and efficiency whilst striving for flexibility, innovation and integration with technology. BPM aims to improve business continuously and was initially developed through a system called Six Sigma pioneered by Motorola in an effort to gain efficient manufacturing practices in the 1950's.

An empirical study of BPM in 2009 by Kohlbacher indicated that BPM creates higher product quality, customer satisfaction, speed of delivery and time to market. This is because BPM allows organisations to abstract business processes from technology infrastructure. It goes beyond automating business, allowing business to respond quickly to changing market, consumer and regulatory demands, a familiar set of challenges where the RDR is concerned.

Along with creating many value and service propositions for the business, understanding the value chain can also highlight the core offering your business brings to the market. If this is understood and marketed correctly, then a powerful voice has been found for the business, which can communicate the uniqueness of the brand and will attract the customers you desire. All brands who understand their core offering are highly successful and sustainable: think Virgin, Lucozade, Boots the chemist (it's even in their title). They all are instantly recognisable in their respective markets for what they do. Armed with this knowledge, your business can become a very powerful brand in the world of the RDR.

11.3 Knowledge:
Over the past 5 years or so, the trend in governance and regulation has been to address the issues surrounding the market and consumers' behaviour. This is evidenced in the consultancy papers written for the FSA, with the 2006 Baseline report documenting the financial capability of the UK population, Thorenson's 2008 review of generic financial advice, University of Bristol's 2008 evidence of financial education levels and impact and David de Meza et al 2008 paper on Behavioural economics.

The application of social science in this way must be applauded. Although there are skeptics when it comes to control group experiments and research, the data and results from the above papers generally includes little research involving students but consists of real life test cases where consumers of financial products (the vast majority of us) behaviour and attitudes are empirically tested. The results are not only interesting but sometimes disturbing, revealing the psychological and cognitive contracts we have with our money and finances. As documented in Chapter 5, government and regulators are quick to employ all sorts of techniques such as gentle encouragement based on such psychological assessment and knowledge attained.

'Myopic loss-aversion' the case for Neuroeconomics

The mental processes that drive financial decision-making some feel those that avoid emotion do better...think Mr Spock from Star Trek...

'Libetarian Paternalism' the term coined by Thaler and Sunstein in their book Nudge, is a good way to sum up how government and regulators view themselves when it comes to encouragement, enforcement or control of consumers' decision making. It is quite clear that the behavioural evidence and risks presented by de Meza and co relating to peoples preference to maintain the status quo, for 'hyberbolic discounting' (short term rather than long term thinking) and financial judgment to be relatively easily affected by 'anchoring' techniques, shows that knowledge of such subjective reactions maybe a valuable commodity in its own right when it comes to both regulation and engagement of financial service organisations and people in general.

Such a scientific approach has also been applied to the regulation of the markets themselves. Evolutionary biology has begun to play a huge part in gaining knowledge on the recent collapse of the financial markets. If the study of organisms is viewed through the lense of the individual verses the group, then scientists have applied such relations to society and financial markets themselves. The idea is that in terms of globalisation and the interconnectivity of markets, we have seen risk either being ignored or defused. With increasing bubbles in the market (e.g. property related sub-prime loans), then this creates a toxic tipping point in the market system. In his book "The Tipping Point', Malcolm Gladwell describes moments in time when products or brands have gained so much momentum that eventually, dependant on the circumstances, nothing can stop their success or collapse. Unfortunately the relaxation of regulation on banks such as the Glasteagle act in the 1980's under Bill Clinton's presidency which removed 'buffers or Chinese walls' between investment and retail banking, created a greater appetite for risk even with depositors' money. Needless to say it ended in near catastrophe for the banking fraternity, investors and the taxpayers.

Systems biology offers the regulators in particular, a way of evaluating how to govern the system rather than the individual entity. This paves the way for guarding against what Gladwell would call a 'superspreader' which generally is a local virus (e.g. HIV) that can spread like wildfire once a tipping point is reached. Where financial regulation is concerned, the virus would be the Lehman brothers' collapse in September 2008 that led to the financial crisis. In reality, the problems were around much earlier and if detected, could have been managed. The regulators could quarantine promiscuous diversifiers and incorporate protection to stop the disease spreading.

A recent example of this is Sir John Vickers interim report for the Independent Commission on Banking (ICB) that suggests "systemically important banks" should hold 10 percent of equity to risk-weighted assets, which is above and over the 7 percent baseline ratio that Basel III stipulates. This report also suggests that such a focus on liquidity will make the 'too big to fail' argument redundant and recommends that banks form separate subsidiaries for retail operations in a bid to protect ordinary savers. This report has effectively stopped short of breaking up the banks, but it does highlight how knowledge of such super-spreader viruses in the financial world, can lead to the creation of ring-fencing of assets to avoid the like again.

Indeed the ICB's report is a follow on from the US Dodd-Frank Wall Street Reform and Consumer Protection Act proposed in 2009, which was commissioned by the Obama presidency to 'promote the financial

Lemarck vs Darwin

Co-operation vs competition: There has been recent interest in Lemarck's theory of co-operation within evolution and its significant role in sustaining life.

stability of the US by improving accountability and transparency in the financial system'.

Such a 'Darwinistic' approach explains much, and can help us understand why markets react the way they do, and if we also apply Jean-Baptiste Lemarck's view of evolution: one of adaptable evolution that responds to the environment and is of an orderly and co-operative nature, then this may lead to the other exertions of scientific principle as applied to economic behaviour. Physioeconomics is a good example where emotional processes that guide economic behaviour are examined, such as heart rates or skin responses (e.g. sweating) that occurs when investment decisions are made.

Indeed Richard Dawkins'[29] theory of mimetics (cultural informational transfer) can also be applied to better understand behavioural economics and the industry and markets themselves. This pertains to show how ideas and influential beliefs or patterns of behaviour may reproduce and populate across society evoking Gladwell's tipping point idea, which in investment market terms may create a herd mentality leading to overheated asset bubbles.

All this may or may not grab your interest, but either way there's no avoiding the fact that whether you're a consumer or a market participant, in an ever more connected world, knowledge is power. In particular knowledge of behavioral economics and how this affects financial decisions most definitely gives a tremendous advantage when deciding where to invest your money or how to design your business and engage with your clientele within the market space in which you operate.

[29] Dawkins Richard, The selfish gene, 1989 Oxford University Press.1-352.

11.4 Pedigree

Knowing where we're going is important, but any attempt to best gauge the most efficient way to get there has to incorporate a clear definition of how the UK financial service market has evolved, enabling us to understand quite why the government and the regulators do what they do. As can be seen from the chapter on behavioural economics, human beings can be both rational and irrational (sometimes at the same time) and this applies equally to the powers that be who set the rules. I have argued in the opening chapter that there has been scant regard for past failed regulation of the markets. Surely the RDR would have been far stronger and well received if a consultation period was held to include a cross section of market participants, academics and government to assess exactly what has gone wrong in the past and the reasons why?

Such an inclusive process may have taken time and cost money, but in the long term a unified approach with buy-in at most levels would aid understanding and willing participation in the transition to fee based advice, professionalisation and consumer education on reasons for the RDR. As I've already suggested, with hyperbolic discounting in mind, maybe the regulators have suffered from a corporate memory loss and forgotten the mistakes of the past. To be fair, the evolution of the regulator itself has been a highly political process with differing governments preferring a certain regulatory approach. During Margaret Thatchers 'Neo-Liberalism' of the late 70's deregulation was key: 'New' Labour's macro-management style established the FSA as an independent regulator from the government and Bank of England (BoE), but this has now already begun to break up with powers being transferred back to the BoE, PRA and the FSA becoming the FCA.

So how can the industry's regulatory and governance genealogy add value going forward? Well it's important to point out that the UK has enjoyed one of the most stable financial service markets in the world, and despite the chopping and changing, we have seen a steady growth in the industry to a position where the industry is now worth an estimated over £9 trillion and employs around 350,000 of the population. London itself became the financial capital of the world and thus the main support for the economy.

Yet with such emphasis on capitalism and macro-management at government level, we have also seen a huge gap created in people's understanding of their own financial capabilities and the investment opportunities laid in front of them. This makes for a dangerous position, as we have seen with the consumer-driven economies flat lining through the financial crisis. By the end of September 2010, total lending to individuals reached over £1,455 billion, of which 84% or £1,222 billion was mortgage lending and the remainder £233 billion was consumer credit (of which £56 billion was secured on credit cards).

Table 11.1: Total individual debts (£ billion)

Individual Debts	1997 (to May)	2010 (to June)
Secured on dwellings	£419	£1,222
Consumer credit	£84	£233
Total	£503	£1,445

SOURCE: Bank of England.

So again we begin to see that regulation needs to incorporate psychology of financial behaviour into the planning process to (at the very least) better understand how to learn from the past and develop an inclusive strategy that informs and educates along with controls. Like it or not, the Big Society is a stab in this direction: we are seeing an emphasis on accountability for all and encouragement of entrepreneurialism with the Big Society bank and its 'social investment market'. Interestingly this organisation will operate independently from the government and will act as a wholesaler, placing investment directly into social enterprises or businesses that operate a social purpose. This alliance of banking with community illustrates how Corporate Responsibility may also play a role in the betterment of financial education both inside and outside the industry.

Corporate Responsibility (CR) has now become integral to business and society alike with legislation such as the Companies Act 2006 keeping CR as a mandatory accounting procedure. CR has been proven to provide reciprocal benefits such as sustainable relations and profitability, productive communications, and stakeholder engagement. In their research, Elisabet Garriga and Dominec Mele (2004)[30] suggest that most CR focuses on the following elements: (a) synergising social demands with business results (b) responsible business, (c) business strategy that produces sustainable profits and (d) contributing to society by doing what is ethically correct. The UK-based CR consultancy "Business in the Community" provides guidelines on corporations reporting on CR strategy and uses a four-part model to frame the relationship between business and society: the marketplace, employees, environment and the community.

So if viewed as an integrative strategy, CR maybe incorporated into regulatory means via education of the public on the affect of their financial behaviour, an undertaking to understand the regulatory mistakes made in the past and a commitment to communicate clearly and engage with all relevant market participants. This will then help create a resolute strategy that can provide benefits for all parties touched by regulatory change.

---

[30] Garriga Elisabeth and Mele Dominec Corporate Social Responsibility Theories: Mapping the Territory, Journal of Business Ethics vol 53 no 1-2 51-71 2004. 71 2004.

11.5 Structure

Adaptability is essential within any industry and none more so now than in the new territory of the RDR. Business must learn quickly to change effectively and efficiently by employing theory and practice and using experience as a guide. As mentioned in Chapter 6 concerning business models, there are plenty of firms who feel they have already met RDR requirements, yet as we do not know the full extent of how the rules may play out, those who sit and wait play a dangerous game.

Successful intermediary business models that employ fee based services are out there, we only have to look at the law firm case study on fee collection to see how this can work in a profitable manner whilst attracting and retaining client support. Although financial services has its own challenges, once a fee structure is understood and in place we then have a position where the ground rules are set, accepted and understood by all participants and the business can move ahead. Yet there is quite clear ambiguity surrounding fee charging and we must gain a clear structure for the ground rules in this area to ensure uniformity and transparency for all.

Decisions around restricted or independent and passive advice are already being taken along with the execution only system by most Bancassurers, IFAs and wealth managers and we are certainly seeing moves within the product providers to begin to court either distribution channel.

A recent survey of 500 IFAs conducted by Skandia showed a majority believed adviser charging to be the main driver behind the focus on structural change, namely client segmentation. Advisers are already segmenting their client bank and yet surprisingly only 27% are incorporating their clients' needs or objectives. A smaller number (4%) are segmenting their clients based on preferences around fees and commissions and a similar amount are segmenting around clients' willingness to pay for advice. By far the largest majority (30%) are segmenting clients based on the size of their portfolios. This in itself indicates that polarisation maybe already in play at the sales end of the industry.

A clear concise structured client segmentation policy driven by the clients' needs and wants should place the business in a strong position going into the RDR. This will reaffirm the firm's commitment to the client and reassure the client that the business places their needs at the heart of its structure.

Back office structure will almost be a deal breaker if underestimated or miscalculated. Advisories, wealth managers, product providers and banks all need to ensure they have

Skandia survey of 500 IFAs

- 59% believed adviser charging to be the main driver behind structural change focus.
- Almost two thirds of advisers are already segmenting their client bank
- Only 27% are incorporating their clients' needs or objectives.
- 4% are segmenting their clients based on preferences around fees and commissions
- 4.5% are segmenting around clients' willingness to pay for advice.
- 30% are segmenting clients based on the size of their portfolios.

the right people, processes and systems in the right place and thus commitment to re-structure or outsource needs to be agreed early in the RDR transition process. For IFAs in particular who choose the restricted route, outsourcing could be a highly beneficial structure in giving access to skills and advice, technical support, and savings on costs such as salary. Outsourcing providers such as Threesixty, Tenet, Simplybiz and Bankhall all offer flexibility in their approach, yet the obvious downside is loss of full independence, yet will clients really demand such? We will have to wait and see.

For advisories, ensuring the right para-planner is in place is essential and just as lawyers with their para-legals and doctors with their paramedics, advisers themselves should ensure they are complicit with all para-planner practices.

Fund and investment platforms offer the obvious benefits of outsourcing to an 'umbrella' type structure that will incorporate all the relevant functions associated with investment procedure and custodianship. Care needs to be taken when we consider the changing landscape associated with charges and costs in relation to bundling and unbundling and rebating which are all yet to fully play out. There are many who think that the platform market may win for a while, but may become a highly competitive market and thus leading to price wars and a loss of faith amongst the industry participants after a while.

That said, platforms are highly popular and make the process of investing and access easier with consolidation of support and banking systems. Re-registration, if supported by the industry, will allow more flexibility within the investment process as it has become clear that one platform or wrap cannot be a one-stop solution for client needs.

The FSA's thematic review carried out in 2010 looked at 33 IFA firms. Although debatable whether this was representative of the industry as a whole, the risks attached to choosing the correct business model and structure are clear to see. Where platforms are concerned, successful integration and supervision will mean clarity around charging and, around fee collection. The choice the regulator has made with regard to remuneration and platforms is open, i.e. product providers at present can still remunerate platforms with a form of rebating, but this maybe closed at some stage in the near future.

Vertical integration mergers and consolidation are already at play in the market place and we are seeing easily recognisable brands merge such as Resolution's successful acquisition of Friends Provident UK, Axa UK Life and Bupa health insurance to create a formidable life and pension company re-branded as Friends Life. Such a company can then pick the distribution channel it sees fit for the market, which may well influence other parties to follow suit. Simple product is such a route.

With an increase in consumer awareness and understanding of the life and pensions sector, the RDR may well place less strain on the sale of life and pension companies, which in turn could lead to healthy competition in the market which can benefit most parties with competitive products and pricing.

11.6. Communication

We all know when mantras are made by politicians they are trying to emphasise a point that will gain traction with their voters. Tony Blair's "education, education, education" is one, David Camerons' follow up was the now very topical 3 letters; "N H S". My '3 Es' are structured around communicating the right values, strategies and ethics where RDR implementation is concerned:

Engage, Enthuse, Enlighten

a) Engage

As we have seen communication of the reasons for and why the RDR is with us has involved a high level of asymmetry and in balance of information and opaque delivery so far. The top down approach can appear to some as 'bayoneting the wounded' in its non-consultative process and thus it's now good to see the TSC and industry professional bodies getting active in championing an open and inclusive advisory strategy.

It is also good to see the FSA now implementing RDR road shows, insurance groups, IFA's and banks offering RDR information via their websites and brochures, professional bodies organising RDR conferences and business consultancies offering bespoke RDR implementation programmes. Such engagement needs to be encouraged from the top if we are to see a comprehensive commitment to the RDR principles. There is plenty of stick with too little carrot, and although the majority of the market participants think the RDR is commendable in principle, practice is entirely another issue.

The chapter on marketing gave 3 ways to engage the chosen market within the new RDR remit: making it easy, personal and normal. Whether a bank, IFA or product provider, using such a strategy will enable consumers to better understand the services or products on offer, making them tangible and user friendly. They could even apply to the regulators.

The engagement of the consumers needs far more focus and work. The FSA has only just released statements for the consumer explaining the RDR at time of writing. Yet this surely is not enough. The industry itself could take this opportunity to once and for all place the consumer at the very heart of their services by offering educational programmes that will gain and nurture their trust.

b) Enthuse

Disturbing the industry and consumer alike to feel animated and invigorated by the RDR principles may seem a difficult task. Yet if the principles are communicated correctly and the objectives of RDR, to deliver standards of professionalism that inspire consumer confidence and build trust so that, in time, retail investment advice is seen as a profession on a par with others. Then the general public will gain a comprehensive understanding of the objectives and this can go a long way to bring a dynamic standard to the acknowledgement and interaction between various market participants.

The 3 RDR Principles:
- A transparent and fairer charging system: Enthuse by communication of the value chain and relationship of the services and TERs to the client. This will empower all parties with greater understanding of the value gained.
- A better qualification framework for advisers: Enthuse through

the professionalisation of the industry (that according to Which? Magazine is a high public priority), and this will inform a higher standard of practice.

- Greater clarity around the type of advice being offered: Enthuse via transparency of communication via the written and spoken word.

c) Enlighten

The work around consumer psychology and financial capability, if used correctly, can galvanize and inspire clients to buy services that are perceived as empowering and educational. As we have seen, social and behavioural sciences all shed light onto interactions that lead people to act in certain ways and techniques we may employ to ensure they are educated to concede, comply and even change their ways.

We just have to employ the principles suggested by David de Meza and co or Bob Cialdini in is his work on influence and persuasion, which advocate the benefits of communicating your liking of others (empathy), reciprocity (give-get), social proof (benchmarking of success), consistency (true to your word), authority (expertise) and scarcity (limiting or simplifying options) as ways of educating your clients and gain following and trust.

It is encouraging to see the Money Guidance scheme now in action, a result of the Thorenson Review on generic financial advice which principles are:

- 'On my side' - delivered by advisers with empathy and clear questioning skills.
- Supportive - providing people with confidence, support and motivation to take specific action.
- Preventative - helping people take charge of their affairs before serious problems develop.
- Universal - Money Guidance appeals to a broad mix of people.
- Sales free - helping people make their own decisions and not directly linked to selling.

Technological change and its application within financial services has come along way since the early days of phone banking (First Direct) and can now do more to aid the education of the consumer within financial services. Surely we must now see technology designed around the clients and not the industry's needs; where an independent financial information and educational resource is built around the clients' subjective needs along with the industry's products and services. We are seeing the (rare) beginning of such advances such as the Consumer Financial Education body's Money Advice Service (the name can deceive), DECODE's work on financial services and Generation Y's co-creation of financial products and websites such as Allmyplans.com. Such advances will mean a re-orientation of communication channels between the industry and consumer. For example clients may build their own financial plans, which are handed back to the adviser for sign off or apply for bespoke products that are generated in an instant online. Investors will also have a say in how the product is structured and online access to banking via social media and conference screening. This is all a possibility.

11.7 Conclusion = Application:

"To boldly go where no man has gone before"

We are at a critical stage with RDR transition where all parties affected need to be confident and committed on their journey to 2013 and beyond. Although we will not know how the landscape will truly look, if business, regulators and consumers alike strike a common chord of communication and mutual engagement towards similar goals, then this may make the path more palatable and create unity not discord.

I have attempted to address numerous issues, some which probably need a book in their own right to fully explore their ramifications. Yet if each and every one is addressed and applied with courage and conviction then we will see some exciting business-to-business, and business to client, relationships being born.

So when it comes to nurturing and maintaining client trust, the regulators and industry have a shared responsibility to ensure the key RDR processes are implemented succinctly and transparently. If we go back to David Maister et al's work on client trust, this is defined by a formula, which gives us an equation to benchmark how much trust we are generating and how this maybe improved. The less self-orientation we are then the more trust is generated.

> **The Trust equation:**
> **Trust** = $\dfrac{C+R+I}{S}$
>
> *Where:*
> C=Credibility
> R=Reliability
> I=Intimacy
> S=Self-orientation
> David Maister, Charles Green & Robert Guildford.

Obviously where Credibility, Reliability and Intimacy are concerned they also fit with Bob Cialdini's principles of influence, particularly liking, social proof and consistency, and David Lamberts' concept of relationship capital. This means that where the RDR is concerned and the comprehensive change management process that goes with it, then there are key areas that, if managed and communicated clearly and client participation is encouraged, then trust and loyalty will most definitely be a result which will ensure a healthy and prosperous relationship for all parties. So what are they?

Technology
In his book "Enchantment", Guy Kawasaki positions two of his chapters to what he calls 'push and pull' technology. What this means is using the like of Twitter, Power point and email to bring your story to people and Facebook, Youtube, Linked-in and blogs to bring people to your story. 🐦#RDRBOOK

I make no apologies for banging the technology drum when it comes to the RDR. Firstly such push and pull applications will aid client awareness and communication of your RDR journey and how your services are positioned to help them post 2013. Whether you are B2B, B2C or B2B2C, it doesn't matter: the same principles apply. You may think I'm stating the obvious, but I'm still surprised by many well-established industry participants who do not utilise such technology in an efficient and effective manner.

Generation Y now demand instant knowledge and data. It has become part of everyday life, particularly with the expansion of the Internet and in particular Google. In their book 'Selling to the C-Suite', Nicholas A.C Read and Stephen J. Bistritz, highlight the fact that selling has systematically shifted the gatekeeper of knowledge from the salesman to the customer thanks to the Internet. This presents a huge challenge to industry and particularly to financial services. Soft skills and the art of communication are therefore now at the forefront of client relations. We can no longer 'hide' behind technical knowledge and product jargon.

In this regard, DECODE's product co-build strategy seems to be on the money for facilitating good understanding and relations between business and the consumer. This is essentially a move away from the consumer being seen by industry as technically incompetent when it comes to investing, and should therefore ensure a reciprocal engagement of education for both parties via the medium of technology where business and consumers learn together: a kind of corporate responsibility if you like. There is much to be said for true client facing technology to be employed and designed for clients' not industry's needs.

The use of social media technology in particular will facilitate quick, clear marketing messages to reach the target audience, and the consumer's needs for easy to understand, fast paced knowledge of products and services will be met. So a well targeted marketing strategy that involves the use of client facing technology will facilitate some of the influence factors we have alluded to such as gaining authority, consistency of message, liking of brand along with reciprocity of information giving and gaining social proof.

There's now getting away from the numbers as the below figures show, intelligent usage of social media technology will give the business a cutting edge relationship with their clients.

Figure 11.1: UK Social Media Usage.

facebook   **26m active users (42% of pop.)**

twitter   **5m active users**

You Tube   **17m active users**

Linked in   **4m active users**

SOURCE: *mrm consultancy.*

Finally, but not least, it's no secret that google, Microsoft, facebook, twitter all have banking licenses of sorts and we are already seeing google opening basic financial services in America: a shot across traditional banking bows maybe?

Efficiency

As we have seen throughout this book, for business to gain the best possible chance of survival in 2013 and beyond, much will depend on the capabilities, competence, and proficiency of their value chains, products and services. There are many areas of interest here, but the most relevant to the consumer are;

Fees

Application of the fee process is one area where we need to ensure the RDR rules are understood and applied by all, thereby ensuring clarity and transparency and healthy competition. The 'commission mindset' that the industry seems to suffer from needs to be put to bed and as our solicitor case study shows, true and transparent application of fee-based services is profitable for all concerned. A fee is just that, remuneration based on time taken to procure advice, and thus moves the emphasis from product to added value time spent as the commodity.

Fee collection needs to be a clear transaction between the advisory and the client and ring-fenced as such. Thus with ICAAP principles in mind, platforms and wealth management businesses may want to employ escrow accounts to protect clients' monies against liquidity of a business.

Remuneration within the advisory industry also needs to be changed. The typical commission based 'hunter' profile is now unacceptable. The "kill and feeding frenzy' stereotype that has plagued the commission-based retail financial planners image can be laid to rest, particularly if professionalisation leads to a salaried position with sensible bonus structures. Even if fees are based on a 'commission only' strategy, then services sold (intermediation), will only be remunerated by those clients who see real value in the services provided.

Charges and pricing
Revenue streams across the value chains needed careful consideration and application. We are already seeing product providers switching to institutionally priced products for all, and with a rebate ban still currently in place on platforms. A re-think on how orphaned clients maybe handled post RDR.

Surely 'big tent pricing' will become extinct with the RDR? As we have seen from the information on platforms and wraps, products will have to move to an unbundled or clear pricing structure, there should be no hiding place for subtle implicit charges.

Risk management
A huge area in its own right, but key issues such as catching,

measuring, mitigating and reducing risk of business operations by employing business process modelling, which will highlight the real costs of risk and gaps in RDR compliance to the business. BPM will provide an evidence-based practice and validation that will give crucial information and data to manage risks as:

- Fair and accurate pricing and charging,
- Efficient processes and services,
- Engagement and maintenance of client relations.

Strategy:

We have explored many of the main areas surrounding the business model, written and verbal communication and change management techniques. Application of an agreed strategy needs to be led and managed with full confidence and inclusion of all relevant parties. Remember the development of Peter Senge's theory around the 'learning organisation' which gives values of a 'flatter' organisation rather than a hierarchical structure: an organisation that learns and transforms itself to remain competitive, innovative, knowledgeable, and engage stakeholder's needs. According to Senge (1990) learning organisations are:

"...organisations where people continually expand their capacity to create the results they truly desire, where new and expansive patterns of thinking are nurtured, where collective aspiration is set free, and where people are continually learning to see the whole together."

Institutional theory has taught us to be confident in our ingenuity and avoid a follow the herd mentality. Herd decisions can affect the end user in dramatic ways. Malcolm Gladwell's social science examines how cultural, social, and economic factors converge to create trends in consumer behaviour sometimes with disastrous consequences. Where financial services are concerned we need look no further than the credit crunch and how entwined banking operational models were to see this.

A key strategy for any change management process is simplicity;

Simplicity

Keep it simple stupid? Well certainly there's much to be said for keeping change and client management issues as simple as possible. There is always the temptation to over-engineer the strategies and desired structures and relationships when if the process is taken in incremental steps whilst remembering to involve the clients within the change management process, then the desired results will come. Remember hyperbolic discounting: to manage risk in change it is surely better to keep track on the longer term objectives whilst making small wins along the way.

Clients will thank the company for informing, engaging and enlightening them on the challenges and goals faced by the RDR, and ultimately will remain loyal and trust the firm's change management strategies, as they will see how client segmentation or client engagement policy benefits them in the longer term.

Remember the marketing strategy of keeping it easy, normal and personable and key factors for understanding judgmental bias and increasing financial capability: education, nudges, defaults, lifestyle budgeting, counter-intuitive strategies. These are all key areas for any organisation taking their clients through substantial change.

Soft Skills

The National Occupational Standards (NOS) promoted by the Financial Skills Partnership, (formally the Financial Services Skills Council) gives plenty of steering and direction around client engagement around the 6 stages process we reviewed in Chapter 2. Yet as mentioned in our chapter on soft skills, a key module completely missed is that which surrounds the engagement and maintenance of client relations in the verbal format. i.e. understanding client behaviours. #RDRBOOK

The emotional intelligence and our body language that surrounds what we say and do and the way we subjectively interact with clients, is now critical in relation to ensuring financial capability, loyalty, trust and support is built and maintained post 2013. At my business consultancy Engage Partnership Ltd, we have devised a whole learning and development programme around this concept 'Better Client Relationships', that is essentially explained by the '3 E's'; **Engage, Enthuse and Enlighten.**

Understanding Client Behaviour: Performance:

Engage:
- Use of technology and social media in marketing and communications.
- Find clients who are suitable for engagement of the services offered.
- Using client segmentation, identify clients who may not need a full services but who will definitely benefit from good quality product or advice.
- Using client segmentation, identify clients who may decide to orphan themselves of services or products at some stage in the future.

Enthuse:
- Communicate and inspire a client into understanding the value of understanding their capabilities and the need to act consistently and in a timely fashion.
- Recognise and counteract a client's inclination to dispense with on-going advice after the third year of a relationship paying a barefaced fee retainer.
- Identify how external and internal events shape behaviour (e.g. environment, cause and effect) and alter clients' beliefs about risk.
- Identify behavioural signals when a client may harbour unvocalised unease about the relationship.

- Identify clients who may default on services or fees or who will naturally stretch out any period of credit.
- Develop a process of identifying clients best suited to simple product or restricted or simplified advice where necessary and refer when appropriate.
- Create a due diligence package for deployment in situations where you are in competition for advice.

Knowledge and Understanding:

Enlighten:
- Educate: on the demographics of services and advice: such as suitability of product, product interventions, kite marking, and simple product or chosen advice strategy.
- Influence & Pursuasion: awareness of the universal factors of influence & persuasion as tempered by ethics, such as work done by Professor Bob Cialdini, Dr Kevin Dutton and others to aid industry understanding of how best to engage clients and educate on financial capability.
- Behavioural economics: as it applies to financial services. The works of David de Meza, Otto Thorenson and the research done and commissioned by the FSA, are important resources to be used as guides to understanding consumer financial capability.
- Ethics: the operation of the court of protection and what is expected of deputies when reporting to the Court. All areas under redress, complaints and compliance.
- Positioning: By placing the emotional cycle alongside the investments cycle, we can see that the two will not necessarily match. Thus as Warren Buffet advocates " Be fearful when others are greedy and greedy when others are fearful" it makes sense to watch emotions just as much as the stock markets.
- Practical application: on job learning, mentoring, role modelling, team ethics, self analysis, networking, learning and development programmes, risk management and incorporating co-creation strategies for product building and use of technology. Framing

and anchoring techniques may then be employed to ensure clients understand their own emotional contract with their finances and key behavioural finance areas such as loss aversion, inertia, status quo bias and hyperbolic discounting can be managed.

An understanding of the behavioural economics and judgmental biases, detailed in Chapter 5, of both consumers and the industry is vital to the inter-action, communications and skill sets needed to garner trust and enhance public financial capabilities.

Transparency
Finally, but not least, the application of transparent solutions is a must for competitive advantage post RDR implementation. This applies right across the value chain, business model, communication and distribution channels.

The word "transparency" appears over 800 times in the FSA literature and more so in governmental communications. You have to look no further than the No 10 website to see a whole section dedicated to transparency and openness in political practice. http://transparency. number10.gov.uk/. True transparency is actually difficult to attain if we take into account the way financial service products have been structured historically. It is difficult to communicate completely what financial institutions are doing with their clients' money and how they are charged through a bundled structure. Yet companies like the online bank EGG and the high street bank the Co-operative attempt to place themselves in their clients' shoes when designing their services. At government level, proposals of simplified legislation surrounding UK pensions and taxation and are all leading the way towards a transparent and easier to understand financial legislative system.

Evidence based practice and management, has shown how data maybe gleaned from the business value chains and used to enable better and informed choices based on empirical evidence. This may be actioned by the business modelling systems we described earlier to enable the organisations to map out their value propositions and ensure they understand why the change needs to happen and how it may be executed. EBM will thus give transparency to the business operations and services across the whole value chain.

Transparency across the value chain of any business will facilitate clear and efficient distribution channels, enable communications to be understood and (in theory) lower redress in the industry due to customer education and knowledge gained by product for example. We have seen how evidence based management of change may actually improve the performance, self-awareness and compliance of an organisation to the RDR principles.

Although the RDR may have been construed more clearly and communicated more inclusively, this regulatory driven measure is going along way to improving transparency in distribution of retail financial services. The RMAR measures are an example of how the regulator will hold the industry participants accountable through (in this case) data collection and supervision on specific activity.

If we truly embrace the RDR principles and sit within the rules surrounding fee charging, professionalisation and clarity on advice and charging then we have firm and ready structures, models and strategies in place that will prove rigorous and flexible enough to transform the business through the RDR challenges and environment that will be shortly upon us. The business will thrive along with customer relations, with clients able to understand the true value of the services on offer and trust the relationship.

Summary

In application of the above TESST principles we have key areas for focus to generate sustainable success and client trust through the RDR change management journey and into the brave new RDR world, which if successful, may actually place the client and their needs at the heart of the business.

Chapter 12
The Trust Factor

"Learning to trust is one of life's most difficult tasks".
Isaac Watts.

We have identified 5 key areas in principles for application (Technology, Efficiency, Strategy, Soft skills, Transparency) that will, if implemented effectively, provide the business and their clients with a cohesive framework through the change management challenges we have discussed. If the business has then spent plenty of time, resource and effort in application of the TESST principles, how will this facilitate and maintain true client loyalty and trust?

12.1 Trust defined

Stephen M.R Covey in his book 'The speed of Trust'[31] simply stipulates you can't have success without trust and quotes Jack Welch former CEO of General Electric who said of trust *"you know when you feel it"*. Covey defines trust as confidence where the opposite is suspicion and builds in 13 required behaviours for relational trust to develop. All good, yet as alluded to in the introduction to this book from my experience within financial services, client trust takes time and is a result of an accumulation of events through a journey taken by willing participants.

David Maister's et al's Trust equation built on the addition of credibility, reliability and intimacy divided by the degree of self-orientation is good, but as this supports the assertion that it's easier to work with people that you have existing relations with (as you have already built levels of credibility, reliability and intimacy) which means that this maybe skewed with new client relations or indeed those relationships that have poor personal chemistry.

David Lambert in the second edition of Smart Selling points to the fact that its therefore good to have a third party involved at some stage or focus on increasing intimacy or empathy with the client which will help reduce self-orientation and resolve this issue.

Where financial services firms are concerned, I believe that the TESST principles, if adhered to and applied, will facilitate a fast and rewarding journey to attain client trust at individual, team, leader or organisation level.

The Trust Matrix best illustrates this.

Figure 12.1: The Trust Matrix

SOURCE: *Engage Partnership Ltd*

The above matrix illustrates the journey to a trusted relationship that the organisation and their clients can choose to take. The ideal area where the highest trust maybe gained is with a transformational relationship which, in DECODE's words, would employ a co-build strategy or, as I call it, a flip-funnel approach where the clients are high in understanding and engagement with the organisation's TESST application.

---

[31] Covey Stephen M. R. 2006. The Speed of Trust. Free Press 1-339.

12.2 The Journey to Trust

As we can see there are four key relations that will affect trust in varying degrees;

Self-Orientation: David Maister's definition is key to this area where organisations or individuals are only concerned with themselves. It is certainly human nature to put ourselves first in relations and difficult to maintain a 'self-free' relationship, particularly in business. The trust matrix graphically illustrates with low client understanding and engagement and the firms lack of application of the TESST principles, this leads to a highly unproductive relationship (sometimes dysfunctional) and where no trust is gained.

Transactional: Where clients hold the upper hand (if they wish) is when they feel empowered by their own knowledge or experience of the industry and feel in control with high understanding and engagement. When industry TESST principles are low in application, then this will lead to a low trust environment where clients will 'cherry pick' products and services again with little or no loyalty or relationship in evidence.

Educational: The areas of behavioural economics and financial capability have shown that government, regulators and industry need to engage the consumer and instill programmes and incentives that will educate on and empower their understanding and engagement of financial needs. As we have seen in Chapter 5 there are strategies that can be introduced quickly and at relatively low cost, yet the issue here is it will take a lot of time and effort from the business to generate client understanding, engagement and then trust. This is a stepping-stone to the next level and must be encouraged by all market participants.

Transformational: Where the 'Trust Factor' lies is when organisations and clients enter a relationship capital of mutual reward and respect. This is often referred to as the 'zone', when relations are effortless, positive, energised, and aligned. This creates high empathy and compliance with David Maister's credibility, reliability and intimacy and means the organisation has applied clear and understandable Technology, Efficiency, Strategy, Soft-skills and Transparency as defined in Chapter 11.

We then begin to see how business can map out their change management objectives and involve clients heavily in the process to facilitate a transformational relationship for both parties. This means a flip funnel approach, where clients needs are placed at the centre of the business, value chains are streamlined and clear and the irrationality and judgmental biases that belies behavioural economics is managed.

12.3 The Trust Factor

Where trust is derived and a transformational relationship is formed, this then allows business freedom to sustain the model and clients to enjoy fair value and healthy exchange. We move away from a give-get 'quid pro-quo' exchange to a flow of enhanced motivation, morale and performance from both parties that moves the self-orientation to a minimalist level and creates high trust for all.

This relationship can become a state of mind and many social scientists have proposed theories of how this is attained, from Abraham Maslow's hierarchy of needs, Victor Vroom's expectancy theory, Edward Deci's self-determination theory, John Adams equity theory to Milhaly Csikszentmihalyi's flow theory. Indeed it is flow theory and equity theory that helps define the 'zone' I have alluded to, in that when individuals are engrossed in demanding activity with high skill levels this leads to a sense of control, time distortion, and high reward. Equity theory suggests people value fair treatment and this creates a reciprocation of fairness in relations. Similarly, with a transformational relationship, the organisation will offer high TESST principles and the clients bring high understanding and engagement.

The only caveat to this is there must be direct and clear feedback given from both parties at all times in order for this state to be sustainable. This is attainable by high empathy. The Trust Factor is then a highly desirable state of mind and relationship, one that will ensure business and their clients remain satisfied with their relationship capital and grow together knowing that a tenable association has been reached.

As the Beatles song goes, it is a "long and winding road that leads me to you door". The journey to the RDR 2013 January 1st door and beyond is not straightforward, and there are many twists and turns ahead. Yet if business can win a trusted relationship with its clients, with application of TESST principles, this will give a firm foundation for sustainable success for all parties involved and facilitate better client relationships, which is an area in its own right, (perhaps another book?).

In finishing I would like to leave you with one for my favourite anecdotes, which for me, sums up what the journey to attaining the trust factor is;

A little girl and her father were crossing a bridge.
The father was worried for his daughter's safety so he asked her:
"Sweetheart, please hold my hand so that you don't fall into the river."
The little girl said: "No, Dad. You hold my hand."
"What's the difference?" asked the puzzled father.
"There's a big difference," replied the little girl. "if I hold your hand and something happens to me, chances are that I may let your hand go. But if you hold my hand, I know for sure that no matter what happens, you will never let my hand go."

In any relationship, the essence of trust is not in its bind, but in its bond. So hold the hand of the person whom you trust rather than expecting them to hold yours...

The fairer sex is always right? I wish you well on your journey.

AFTERWORD

Congratulations on reading this book

I truly hope you have found the journey the UK retail financial services industry and their clients are now walking and the changes now underway at the very heart of the investment services market, an interesting and thought-provoking read.

You may decide to re-read the book in the context of digging deeper into the story behind the content or in applying strategies to increase consumers' financial capabilities for example.

There are many issues which are also important to the book's themes and points raised, yet it was not possible to include in-depth within the timeframe I had set myself to write the book. The debates that surround taxation and potential polarisation need to be expanded upon, and there is certainly another book to be written surrounding the experiences of industry post 2013 when the RDR becomes a reality.

The book was not just written as a view on the RDR and challenges and opportunities this gives, but as a guide to why the industry is where it is, incorporating the underlying psychological patterns and stories that make up an intriguing blend of behaviour and strategy that play out against the dynamics of the investment market.

I would welcome any comments and ideas around improving financial capability in particular, so please feel free to comment on the books twitter stream #RDRBOOK.

About The Author

Chris has worked within the financial service sector both domestically and internationally for over 20 years, and has enjoyed various roles working within domestic banking, insurance and as an independent financial adviser, sales director and independent consultant.

In the UK, Chris worked with Nat West bank then moved into insurance with Endsleigh insurance group and then Friends Provident First Call managing sales teams and developing and implementing training and competence programmes. In 1996 Chris moved to Hong Kong to further his career as an independent financial adviser with (at the time) the UK's and Asia's leading wealth management group, Towry Law. Chris left Towry to set up his own consultancy and gained contracts with Axa to help implement and develop Asia's first fee based financial planning firm, ipac financial planning, a company that still thrives today.

After 11 years, it was time to repatriate to the UK with a young family in tow, where Chris has been working in a management consultancy capacity. He co-founded engage partnership limited, a financial services focused consultancy, providing strategic planning and support to financial services companies in particular with change management and coaching services along with customer facing technology and software development to meet the ever challenging industry demands.

Chris is ICA: UK trained in group facilitation methods and provides freelance work as facilitator and speaks at industry conferences. Chris is a certified financial planner and holds a Bachelor of English Literature degree from the University of Manchester and a MSc at Birkbeck University London in Organisational Behaviour.

Chris' interests include acting and most sports including marathon running, football and tennis and enjoys reading, writing and theatre.

Additional Resources

1. Key FSA Consultancy and other relevant papers:

http://www.fsa.gov.uk/Pages/Library/Policy/CP/index.shtml

There are many consultancy and discussion papers held on the above FSA website and other related sites and most are well researched and well structured and provide invaluable resource for financial organisations and individuals holding the relevant regulatory permissions in their field of expertise.

I have listed below the key papers that helped with my private clients in their RDR change management programmes and for research for this book.

Adviser charging

CP11/3 Product disclosure retail investments – changes to reflect RDR Adviser Charging and to improve scheme disclosure.

ABI guidance for determining the VAT liability of Adviser Remuneration.

Basic & Primary Advice

CR 70 Consumer Perceptions of Basic Advice.

CR 71 Primary Advice: Consumer perceptions of the Primary advice concept.

Behavioural Economics and Consumer financial capability

Financial capability in the UK, Establishing a baseline.

CR 47 Levels of Financial capability in the UK: Results of a Baseline Survey.

CR 60 Evaluation of the FSA financial capability training for youth work professionals.

CR 69 Financial Capability: A Behavioural Economics Perspective.

CR 68 Evidence of impact: An Overview of financial education evaluations.

DP 08/5 Consumer responsibility.

Financial Capability: developing the role of generic financial advice.

Thorenson Review of generic financial advice: final report.

The Money Guidance Pathfiner: key findings and lessons learned.

Young people & money: A free training programme to help practitioners help 'not in education, employment or training' (NEET) young people make sense of money.

CR 83 Consumer awareness of the FSA and financial regulation.

Consultancy papers

Association of British Insurers Quarterly Consumer Curvey, 2010 Q4-2608 Consumers.

Aviva Report June 2011. The Value of Financial Advice. 1-12.

Barclays Wealth Insights, Volume 13: The Role of Control in Financial Decision Making. In co-operation with Ledbury Research.

Capital financial software: White paper: 'Platforms – big issues and big solutions'.

Deliotte and Touche LLP: Costing Intermediary Services; Financial Assessment of Investment Intermediaries.

Engage Partnership Ltd: The Retail Distribution Review: A transparent solution or opaque reality?

Ernst & Young Business report 2010; The top 10 risks for business.

Investment management association (IMA); Asset management in the UK 2009-2010.

Ernst & Young: Life and Pensions outlook for 2011.

JP Morgan: The Retail Distribution Review: The challenge and the opportunity for wealth managers.

JP Morgan: Adviser Charging: putting the price on financial advice.

KPMG:

Oxera: Retail Distribution Review proposals: Impact on market structure and competition.

Ethics
CP 10/12 Competence and Ethics.

FSA Strategy

Business plan 2011/12

Operational

PS 11/6 The Client Money and Asset Return (CMAR): Operational Implementation.

CP 11/8 Data collection: Retail Mediation Activities Return and complaints data.

Organisational

CP 06/9 Organisational systems and controls.

Platforms

DP 07/2 Platforms: the role of wraps and fund supermarkets.

DP10/02 Platforms: delivering the RDR and other issues for discussion.

CP 10/29 Platforms: Delivering the RDR and other issues for platforms and nominee-related services.

OP 40 Regulating platform charges.

Professionalisation

PS 11/1 Distribution of retail investments: Delivering the RDR – professionalism.

Risk

Financial risk outlook 2010

Retail Conduct Risk Outlook 2011

Assessing suitability: Establishing the risk a customer is willing and able to take and making a suitable investment selection. Paper 1 January 2011, paper 2 March 2011.

Retail Distribution Review

PS 10/6 Distribution of retail investments: Delivering the RDR – feedback to CP 09/18 and final rules.

CP 10/14 Delivering the RDR: Professionalism, including its applicability to pure protection advice, with feedback to CP09/18 and CP09/31

Simple Product
HM Treasury Simple financial products: a consultation.

RDR Rules
Last but not least a must for all market participants under the RDR remit of changes is the rules themselves. They can be found at:
http://fsahandbook.info/FSA/html/handbook/COBS/6
P.s. don't forget to set the date to 1 January 2013...

2. Relevant and interesting organisations and websites
All My Plans:
www.allmyplans.com
Associations British Insurers:
www.abi.org.uk
Association of Independent Financial Advisers:
www.aifaffwd.net
Bright Talk:
www.brighttalk.com
Chartered Insurance Institute:
www.cii.co.uk
Confederation of British Industry:
www.cbi.org.uk
DECODE:
www.decode.net
Financial Ombudsman Service:
www.financial-ombudsman.org.uk
Financial Services Authority RDR:
www.fsa.gov.uk/pages/About/What/rdr/index.shtml
Financial Services Forum:
www.thefsforum.co.uk
Financial Skills Partnership:
www.financialskillspartnership.org.uk
HM Treasury:
www.hm-treasury.gov.uk

Institute of financial planning:
www.financialplanning.org.uk

Investment Management Association:
www.investmentfunds.org.uk

Money Supermarket:
www.moneysupermarket.com

Money Savings expert:
www.moneysavingsexpert.com

PanaceaIFA:
www.panaceaifa.com

Personal Finance Education Group:
www.pfeg.org

Social Market Foundation:
www.smf.co.uk

Tax Incentivised Savings Association:
www.tisa.uk.com

The Financial Adviser School:
www.thefaschool.co.uk

The National Skills Academy:
www.nsafs.co.uk

The Money Advice Service:
www.moneyadviceservice.org.uk

The personal finance society:
www.thepfs.org

The Platforum:
www.theplatforum.com

Thought Leadership Live:
www.thoughtleadershiplive.com

Xdelia:
www.xdelia.org

Young People and Money:
www.ypam.org

3. Glossary of terms

ABI: Association of British Insurers.

AC: Adviser Charging.

Affect Heuristics: Current affect influences decisions e.g. Rule of thumb.

Accumulation units: Income re-invested for future growth.

Allocation Rates: Percentage of initial investment that goes towards the final investment i.e. net of fees.

APPG: All Party Parliamentary Group.

Anchoring: Over reliance on specific information to govern the thought process e.g. price.

Ancillary Services: Necessary support services.

APR: Annual percentage rate. A year's worth of interest payments.

Asymmetry: One party has greater insights or knowledge than another.

Basel I: 1988 'Basel Accord' set by international central bankers to set minimum capital requirements for Banks.

Basel II: Pillar I capital allocation risk, II operational & credit risk III reduce regulator arbitrage.

Basel III: Pillar I transparency, Pillar II Governance & risk, Pillar III capital requirements.

Basic advice: Delivers simple products (e.g. stakeholders) in cost effective way.

Basis Points (Bps): Percentage charge that fund managers take as remuneration.

Behavioural Economics: Social science related to behavioural finance to understand economic decision making of individuals and institutions.

Big 5 Personality traits: 5 broad dimensions of personality; openness, conscientiousness, extraversion, agreeableness, and neuroticism.

Big Society: Power disinvested from central government used to empower the local people and communities.

Black Box treatment: Tendency to mystify and bundle together information technology.

Bounded rationality: Decision-making is limited by the information to hand, limitations of the mind and time it takes to make decisions.

Bundling/Unbundling: Combined or non-combined charging or product sales.

Buridan's Ass: Paradox in concept of free will named after 14th century French philosopher Jean Buridan.

CAR: Customer Agreed Remuneration.

CBU: Conduct Business Unit. Supervisory and Risk management regime with 4 divisions. Supervisory, Conduct policy, Markets, Authorisations.

Charges Access Terms: CAT standards were introduced regarding the sale of individual savings accounts - ISA's designed to give consumers an at-a-glance guide to product features and benefits. Superseded by Stakeholder products.

Cloud Computing: Computer network that holds resources (data and software).

CMC: Computer Mediated Communication.

COBS: Conduct of Business Sourcebook.

Cognitive System: Knowledge and information processing brain functions.

CPMA: Consumer Protection and Markets Agency. Covers firms not under PRA now incorporated into the FCA.

Customer Charter: Commitment to principles of business.

Default Options: Options given on investment products.

DFM: Discretionary Fund Manager.

Diagnostics: Tools and systems to analyse and interpret behaviour and thinking patterns.

EBM: Evidence based management is best evidence in management decision making, as per Denise Rousseau definition.

Emotional Intelligence: Ability to detect and control the emotions pf self, others and of groups.

Endowment Effect: The value of a commodity is greater once it's owned.

Escalation Fallacy: Throwing good money after bad.

Escrow account: Where a trusted third party may receive and send monies for transacting parties.

Execution only: Investments made without advice.

Factoring: Products advancing adviser charges.

Factory Gate Pricing: Manufacturers price of products or goods.

Flip Funnel: Relationship seen from an 'outside-in' approach, e.g. client to business.

Framing: A collection of stereotypes relied upon to understand and respond to events.

Grandfathering: A Clause that will allow the transfer for older rules to existing situations. In other words to grant an exemption normally for a limited time frame and circumstances.

FCA: Financial Conduct Authority. Consumer protection with prudential responsibility for 25,000 firms sharing a further 2000 with the PRA.

FIMBRA: Financial Intermediaries, Managers and Brokers Regulatory Association Ltd.

Fundamental attribution error: Tendency to over value dispositional (personality) based explanations for behaviours of others.

Generation Y & Z: A western term given to the millennial generation (Y) and Internet generation (Z).

Hard skills: Tangible teachable abilities that lend to performance only.

Hedonic editing: Segregation of multiple outcomes so to achieve the highest value.

Hindsight Bias: Events that have already occurred are seen as more predictable than before they took place.

Heuristics: Decisions made on past experience.

HMRC: Her Majesties Revenue and Customs.

Hyperbolic Discounting: Favouring short term over long term gains.

ICAAP: Internal Capital Adequacy Assessment Process introduced under Basel II for pillar I minimum capital requirements, stress testing techniques, appropriate risk management.

ICB: Independent Commission on Banking.

I-E: Income minus expenses taxation method for life companies.

IMA: Investment Management Association.

IMRO: Investment management regulatory organisation.

Inertia: Resistance to change.

IFA: Independent financial adviser.

Initial Units: Higher charges are applied for an initial period to an investment (normally regular investments).

Institutional Theory: Considers processes by which organisations become established as authoritative guidelines for social behaviour.

Investments cycle: Fluctuations in investment activity, performance and pattern over stages.

ISD: Investment Services Directive: Introduces regulatory harmonisation that allows transfer of services between EU countries with focus on mutual recognition.

Jam Experiment: Social science study on choice preference. The more limited the choice the more motivated consumers are to purchase.

Kite marked product: SMF initiative that can give financial products a quality certification mark.

LAUTRO: The Life Assurance and Unit Trust Regulatory Organisation.

Learning Organisation: Company that continuously transforms itself.

Libertarian Paternailsm: Help in making choices without infringing greatly on freedom of choice.

Limbic System: Supports functions of the brain such as emotion, behaviour and long-term memory.

Locus of Control: The extent to which individuals believe they have control over events that affect them.

Mental accounting: Process of coding, categorising and evaluate economic outcomes.

MiFID: Markets in Financial Investments Directive. Maximum Harmonising EU investment services regulation with emphasis on home state supervision.

MIB: Marketing Investments Board.

Mimetic Isomorphism: The tendency of organisations to imitate another's structure.

Modern Portfolio Theory: Investment theory that maximises

Myopic: Short-sighted.

National Occupational Standards: Statements on performance standards individuals must achieve within the workplace underpinning knowledge and understanding.

NEST: National Employment Savings Trust, to be introduced October 2012.

Neuroscience: Scientific study of the nervous system.

Neuroeconomics: The field that seeks to explain human decision-making. In particular to process multiple alternatives and choose an optimal outcome.

Nudge policy: Active engineering of choice architecture.

OEICS: Open-ended Investment companies are open-ended investments with prices linked directly to underlying investments.

Passporting: As part of MiFID directives, an investment firm can offer services to other participating EU countries.

PBU: Prudential Business Unit 5 Divisions: UK Banks & Building Societies, Investment Banks and Overseas Banks, Insurance, Risk Specialists, Policy.

PRA: Prudential Regulatory Authority. Prime supervisory regime currently being formulated.

PIA: Personal Investment Authority.

Platform: An all-encompassing repository for financial investment products.

Planning Fallacy: Underestimation of length of time it takes to complete a task.

Polarisation: Introduced in 1986 to define the roles of financial services agents giving advice.

PRIPS: Packaged Retail Investment Products.

Professionalisation: Industry move to transform itself into a true profession of the highest integrity and competence.

QCF: Within the National Qualifications Framework (NQF) sits the vocational Qualifications and Credit Framework (QCF), which is the Government's new framework for recognising vocational achievement through the award of units and qualifications.

Rebates: A reduction, return or refund of premium or investment as an incentive for product sales.

RECAP: Record, evaluate and compare alternative prices calls for consumers to have clear information on charges and costs of services and products.

Relationship Capital: Value of individual's worth in the market place.

Representativeness Heuristic: Best described by the famous LINDA experiment, a description of a female as a feminist was given to study participants, they were asked to evaluate the probability of her being a feminist, bank clerk or both. 85% went for the latter. i.e. individuals tend to judge based on information attained.

RIPS: Retail Investment Products.

Risk Profiling: Analysis of client risk appetite and tolerance.

RIY: Reduction in yield, details the effect of total charges on an investment policy.

ROI: Return on investment, a performance measure to evaluate the efficiency of an investment or benchmark against other investments.

RMAR: Retail Mediated Activities Return.

RU 64: Requires an adviser to explain to a customer in writing why the personal pension they are recommending is suitable compared to a stakeholder pension.

Segmentation: Identification of subsets of clients within a market that share similar needs, behaviours or economic worth.

Self-Regulation: A form of self-policing or auto regulation.

SIB: Securities and Investments Board.

Simple product: Vanilla, straightforward and transparent options for financial products.

Simplified advice: Concept based on 'primary advice', which potentially gives plain and fettered advice to the potential mass market that may not partake in independent advice or restricted advice. Yet to be fully defined or implemented.

SIPP: Self-Invested Personal Pension.

Skin in the game: Warren Buffet's idea in which stakeholders all take a financial stake in their business interests.

Social Capital: Societal goodwill which aids social cohesion.

Social Media: Media used for social interaction.

Soft Skills: Personality traits, social graces, communication, language, habits, friendliness, optimism that characterise relationships with people.

Solvency I & II: Introduced in the early 1970's as a risk management system for insurance firms, now developed into a comprehensive 3 pillar strategy based on capital requirements, governance and risk management and disclosure and transparency requirements.

SRO: Self-Regulatory Organisation.

Stakeholders Standards: Charge capping and risk controlled products.

Status Quo bias: Preference to maintain the current equilibrium.

Superspreader: A higher toxic or infectious agent that quickly spreads the infection to other agents with significant effects.

Systems Biology: Bioscience research that focuses on inter-actions in biological systems. This has recently gained attention in respect to the 2008 financial crises and the inter-connected world of finance.

TER: Total Expense Ratio, detailing the total fund costs minus fund assets.

Trails: Regular Remuneration taken at agreed intervals from investment products.

Unit Trust: Pooled investments in stocks and shares where units are bought at offer price and sold at bid price i.e. the Bid-offer spread.

Value Chain: Organisations operational activities and processes.

Vertical Integration: Management control normally through a common owner of supply chains to satisfy a common need.

Wrapper: Also known as a 'wrap account' similar to platform in offering a repository for viewing in one place normally over the Internet.

Y2K: Year 2000 digital and data storage problem resulting from abbreviating a 4-digit year to two digits.

4. Treasury Select Committee Fifteenth Report:

The Retail Distribution Review, summary and comments.

Treasury Select Committee –TSC RDR report	TSC OPINION	Comments
1. Level 4 qualifications and 'grandfathering'.	FSA argument for level 4 is weak. Nevertheless there is some merit in move to higher qualifications. Cliff-edge nature of RDR & ban on Grandfathering could be mitigated with 12 month extension to deadline i.e. January 2014. Supervision of unqualified advisers an option as TSC are concerned at potential loss of expertise.	There is no doubt that higher qualifications in any profession can only be a good thing. I would not argue for a longer lead in period, so I do not agree with the TSC view on a 12 month delay to the RDR implementation despite the FSA's determined stance for 2013 RDR start. Supervision is always an excellent approach to be encouraged within the industry with mentoring and coaching no matter what the experience of qualification levels. There's still time for the FSA to change their mind, for e.g. the Australian regulators had a change of heart of rebating in the late 1990's.
2. Commission.	Customer Agreed Remuneration (CAR) may create a market price for advice Problem is with customers viewing advice as free under commission arrangements thus setting of a price for advice may lead to reduction in consumption. Yet this may also increase customer scrutiny in advice. Trail commission needs to include advice and impact analysis needed on removal of trails. Industry needs to guard against increase in trail up to RDR deadline, currently 2013. Factoring to be banned and TSC agree with FSA.	As stipulated in chapter 6, the CAR involves shades of a 'commission mindset' and such a 'hangover' should be avoided by contemplation of the 'bare faced fee'. Due consideration of ICAAP rules and ring-fencing the client monies need to be addressed by the TSC with escrow accounts in place to protect client monies against liquidation or other adverse circumstances. Trail commissions are essential to advisories thus need to be protected yet evidence that advice is being given and clients paying trail are serviced. Again imagine the perfect storm, we have a market crash, trails collapse, yet fees remain consistent.
3. Level Playing Field.	RDR is for all retail providers i.e. banks as well as advisers. FSA (FCA) to report after one year and annually thereafter on RDR impact on vertically integrated firms' remuneration structures. This is to cover any potential breaches. Transparency is key to ensure the IFA community can evidence it is not unfairly impacted by the RDR.	It is essential to understand that the RDR is potentially beneficial to all retail market participants, thus the current loss of Barclays, HSBC and now CO-OP advisors and bank focus on platform only models maybe a 'knee jerk' and premature reaction. IFA's may still benefit from banks withdrawal as long as transparency on RDR impact is evidenced as fair for all.
4. VAT	Confusion abounds on when VAT is and isn't payable and how much it will raise the cost of advice. TSC recommend the HMRC and FSA liaise with them on when payable and why it has not in the past. This along with additional revenues and whether further reform is needed are essential for clarity on impact on advice.	My consultancy Engage Partnership Ltd are already working with the HMRC to bring definition to the VAT issues. As we have seen with cases such as insurance wide vs HMRC, which illustrate that intermediation tied to product is non VAT-able. (Chapter 8).

5. Types of advice.	Confusion may abound with customers around independent vs restricted advice. Public information needs to be made available on such distinction and in particular that restricted may mean restricted by product or by firm. Simplified advice should be championed and has potential to serve the 'mass market'. This may involve straightforward products and services, highly automated with internet-based offerings. Qualification standards need definition.	Advisers are already determining where they are taking their advice business models. Regulatory arbitrage is a factor where non-advice (execution only) is concerned and we are already seeing IFA's and life companies moving towards this route. Restricted advice needs careful consideration as does simplified advice to potentially facilitate advice to the mass market. Does this mean that such distribution channels can then facilitate level 3 qualified advisers?
6. Transition.	Adverse incentives such as commission leverage and increased trail pre RDR implementation need to be avoided. Pre-implementation churning and post implementation holding of clients (where it is not appropriate) need to be pre-empted by the regulator.	Obviously it would be detrimental to the longer term industry/client relationships if increased trail or commissions were to be taken before January 2013. Behavioural economics need to be understood with hyperbolic discounting to be managed.
7. Costs and benefits.	Overall the RDR aims are laudable yet there maybe some market capacity loss with advisers non compliance. The potential reduction in adviser numbers may disadvantage savers by reducing cost and competition. Regular reports on adviser levels are needed and a 12 month delay to RDR implementation will aid those advisers wishing to remain in the industry and temper the cliff-edge nature of the RDR and required qualifications.	Issues that need to be addressed are product providers factory gate pricing and will a reduction in supply initially raise costs. Where adviser charging is concerned a 'price for advice' will initially be set, but there should be a period of trail and error before a realistic level is reached and clients become attuned and comfortable with fee based advice.
8. European and international issues.	FSA should act to remove consumer detriment in financial services. The risk at present is on 'front running' Brussels with the EU PRIPS initiative which is yet to be fully defined and with no implementation date. Passporting may seem to be an opportunity for advisers to counter the RDR objectives, Yet the FSA is clear that host state standards prevail and cannot be undermined or evaded. FSA to be vigilant on this issue. Where High Net Worth (HNW) individuals are concerned they may not want to participate in RDR requirements, thus FSA need to define direction of any modifications (e.g. opt outs) as necessary for HNW investors.	The fact that Australia are adding insurance into their regulatory regime remuneration changes and Holland is approaching their regulation of financial services in a 'RDR' way means the UK is not alone as the TSC seem to think. Where Europe is concerned, the PRIPS initiative seems to be garnering increased support and with pension reform (similar to UK's) there is a consensus for more interventionist regulation to encourage increased professionalisation and aid better financial capabilities for the consumer.
9.FCA.	FCA will have different objectives to the FSA and thus the Treasury needs to understand and state its contentions as to whether the RDR is consistent with the FCA objectives. Accountability of the FCA needs definition, particularly with vague nature of FSA accountabilities. Long-stop needs addressing and the committee on the Draft Financial Services Bill should consider if long-stop has a place in redress process. TSC believe long-stop would need to evidence consumer interest.	There is no doubt the regulator needs to be accountable. The TSC must be commended for its work so far on the suitability of the RDR reforms and the protection of market participants (e.g. IFA's) in the unintended consequences as documented in chapter 1.

5. FSA Paper PS11/9 Platforms

	Key issues	Comments
1. Overview	1. Payments by providers to platforms 2. Cash rebates to clients.	**CP10/29** wanted to enhanced transparency and disclosure on these payments but with no direct ban (see page 116). A ban was due though on cash rebates to clients. The position has changed to the extent that the FSA wish to ban both outright come Jan 1st 2013, but with work carried out by TISA and other industry bodies, the FSA will take further consultation with any ban starting no earlier than this date. N.b the Aussie regulators did a 180 degree U turn on rebates and allowed them to continue!
2. Defining a platform and distributing products.	1. CP10/29 defined platforms and service providers. Yet question marks remained over providers such as SIPPs/ISAs/CIS/AFMs & if Execution only applied to new definition. 2. Adviser Charging; to gain momentum on platforms, through cash a/cs. 3. Adviser firms use of platforms	1. **PS11/9** defines ISAs as platforms but Life co's, SIPPs CIS, AFMs are not.i.e. those arrangements offered by private client investment managers that are adviser paid and ancillary are not incl. **Execution-only** is included to the extent that **COBS 6.1E.1R** requires disclosure to client of remuneration. i.e. best practice applies. 2. Adviser Charging on platforms to follow product charging as per **COBS 6.1B.9R i.e obtain and validate client instruction.** Funding and servicing of client accounts need to be monitored and in clients best interests. (e.g. if client orphans themselves) **BUT** there is no mention of escrow accounts or indeed ICAAP rulings! (Page 180). 3. Independence standards need to be met when ensuring platforms are right for clients. i.e. no bias and restriction on platform recommendations. **COBS 6.1E.1R**=transparency of fee. Thus care needs to be taken with DFM/supermarkets that need not confirm? Single platform use depends on the clients interests.
3. Payments to platforms and consumers	1. Product providers to platforms CP10/29 addresses potential conflict of interest here and recommend disclosure but no ban. 2. Cash rebates product providers to clients; Rebating seen as a style commission 'throw back'	1. Unbundling seems to be preferred in this paper with proposed ban on product provider payments in order to separate product and platform charges. The RDR objectives of consumer clarity of product charges therefore needs to be upheld. BUT before the ban maybe upheld, impact analysis needs to e completed. 2. Ban to go ahead. The objections to CP10/12 re cash rebating aiding fees, exactly the behaviour FSA want to cull. RDR rules stipulate that client, adviser and providers agree the cost of advice thus this may vary and rebates cannot cope with this and set by provider.
4. Re-registration and capital adequacy.	1. in-specie re-registration standards to be recommended to all nominee companies. 2. COBS 6.1G.1R re-drafted to reflect that not all firms maybe nominee based. 3. Re-registration to take place in reasonable time frame. 4. Share classes and bulk trfrs	The work conducted by TISA and the platform re-registration panel is to be commended and works well with the papers emphasis on ensured best practice and best advice for clients wanted independence of choice and transparency in comparison of available platforms features and benefits. Re the issue on share classes the ban on cash rebates does not mean a proliferation in share classes due to unit re-investment allowance. Re Bulk trfrs most platforms should facilitate re-registration, they're big enough!
5. Investing in authorised funds through nominees.	1. Platform investors to have same access to funds as direct investors. 2. Key Investor Information KII a and associated costs of information for clients.	It is the general industry view the platforms have a rosy future and thus more business will be written and more funds available on platforms. Electronic fund information is to be encouraged with hyperlinks to repository of information on relevant fund information. Short reports as used in UCITS IV are to be recommended i.e. synthetic risk and reward indicator (SRRI) as part of KII. Short forms to be provided 1/4rly. Clients to be kept informed and engaged as is currently on voting rights i.e. CP10/29 proposals cancelled. BUT with key guidelines.
6. Cost benefits analysis.	• Decrease in platform compliance costs from £174.6m to £103.8M (due to rebate ban) • One off cost £55.4m (platforms £40.4, £2.9 fund mgers, £12.1 intermediate fund holders). • Ongoing Costs £48.4m (£20.4 platforms, £28 intermediary fund holders –non for fund managers)	What we need to watch out for and that is not factored in to the cost benefit analysis is the fact that advisers may increase their fees in accordance to the 'missing rebates'.

Bibliography

Abrams Dan. 2011
    Man Down: Proof beyond reasonable doubt that women are
    better cops, drivers, gamblers, spies, world leaders, beer
    tasters, hedge fund managers and just about anything else.
    Abrams Books. 1-144.

Adams, J.S. 1965.
    Inequity in social exchange. Adv. Exp. Soc. Psychol.
    62:335-343.

Argyris Chris (1992)
    On organizational learning. Oxford: Blackwell.

Arierly Dan 2009.
    Predictably Irrational. Harper Collins 1-353

Association of British Insurers Quarterly Consumer Curvey, 2010
    Q4-2608 Consumers.

Aviva Report June 2011.
    The Value of Financial Advice. 1-12.

Barclays Wealth Insights,
    Volume 13: The Role of Control in Financial Decision Making.
    In co-operation with Ledbury Research. 1-24

Barsh. J. 2008.
    Innovation Management. The McKinsey Quarterly;
    Strategy No 1. 1-10.

Bazerman, Max,
    Katherine Milkman and Dolly Chugh How can decision-making
    be improved?

Bennis Warren G. 1969.
    Organisational Development: Its Nature, Origins and
    Prospects. Addison-Welsey Publishing company

Borini, S et al. 2010.
    Rebuilding Corporate Reputations. The McKinsey Quarterly;
    Strategy Practice. 1-8.

Burnes Bernard. 2004.
Kurt Lewin and the planned approach to Change A Re-appraisal. Journal of Management Studies.
41:6. 977-1002.

Capita White Paper: 2010
Platforms – big issues and big solutions. 1-16.

Cialdini Robert.
Influence; Science and mechanics.

Collins, James, C. 2001.
Good to Great. Williams Collins.

Consumer financial education body 2010
The Money Guidance Pathfinder: Key finding's and lessons learned. 1-24.

Covey Stephen M. R. 2006.
The Speed of Trust. Free Press 1-339.

Csikszentmihalyi M.1990.
Flow, The Psychology of Optimal Experience.
New York: Harper and Row. 1-80

Dawkins Richard,
The Selfish Gene, 1989 Oxford University Press.1-352.

DiMaggio, Paul and Powell, Walter. 1983.
The Iron Cage Revisited: Institutional Isomorphism and Collected Rationality in Organisational Fields. American Sociological Review. Vol 48, No 2, 147-160.

Dugdale Keith and Lambert David.
Smarter Selling FT-Pearson Hall.

Dutton David. 2010.
Flipnosis, The Art of Split-Second Persuasion. Arrow Books. 1-381

Eisenhardt, K 1988.
Agency-and Institutional Theory explanations: The case of the retail sales compensation. Academy of Management Journal, Vol 31, No 3, 488-511.

Engage Partnership Limited.
> The Retail Distribution Review an opaque reality or transparent solution? 1-54

Financial services Authority 2005
> Financial Capability Developing the role of generic financial advice. 1-24.

Financial Services Authority 2006.
> Financial Capability in the UK: Establishing a Baseline. 1-28.

Financial Services Authority Consumer 2006
> Research 47 Levels of Financial Capability in the UK: Results of a baseline survey. 1-150.

Financial Services Authority Consultation Paper 06/9
> Organisational systems and controls. 1-272.

Financial Services Authority Consumer Research 68. 2008.
> Evidence of impact: An overview of financial education evaluations. 1-92.

Financial Services Authority Discussion Paper 08/5
> Consumer Responsibility. 1-45.

Financial Services Authority Consumer research 70 2008
> Consumer perceptions of Basic Advice. 1-41.

Financial Services Authority Consumer Research 71 2008
> Primary Advice consumer perceptions of the primary advice concept. 1-31.

Financial Services Authority Consumer research 83 2010
> Consumer awareness of the FSA and financial regulation. 1-84.

Financial Services Authority Discussion paper 10/2
> Platforms: delivering the RDR and other issues for discussion. 1-38.

Financial Services Authority Consultancy paper 10/29
> Platforms: Delivering the RDR and other issues for platforms and nominee-related services. 1-87.

Financial Services Authority Consultation Paper 10/22
> Quarterly Consultation no 26. 1-213.

Financial Services Authority Guidance consultation January 2011
Assessing Suitability: Establishing the risk a customer is willing and able to take and making a suitable investment selection.

Financial Services Authority Guidance consultation March 2011
Assessing Suitability: Establishing the risk a customer is willing and able to take and making a suitable investment selection. 1-31.

Financial Services Authority Discussion Paper 11/1
Product Intervention. 1-75.

Financial Services Authority Policy Statement
Distribution of retail investments: Delivering the RDR – professionalism. 1-126.

Financial Services Authority Consultancy Paper 11/3
Product Disclosure. Retail investments-changes to reflect RDR Adviser Charging and to improve pension scheme disclosure. 1-74.

Financial Services Authority Policy Statement 11/6
The Client Money and Asset Return (CMAR): Operational Implementation. 1-38

Financial Services Authority Consultancy Paper 11/8:
Data Collection, Retail Mediated Activities Return –RAMR.

Financial Services Authority Consultancy Paper 69. 2008.
Financial Capability: A Benhavioural Economics Perspective. De Meza David, Irlenbusch Bernd, Reyneirs Diane, London Scoll of Economics.

Financial Services Authority Retail Risk Outlook 2011. 1-96.

French Wendell L. Bell,Jr. Cecil H. 1999.
Organisational Development, New edition Barnes and Noble. 1-324

Garriga Elisabeth and Mele Dominec 2004
Corporate Social Responsibility Theories: Mapping the Territory, Journal of Business Ethics. Vol 53 no 1-2 51-71.

Gladwell M, 2001.
The Tipping Point, The Story of Success, Penguin Books.

Goldberg Lewis R. 1990.
An Alternative "Description of personality": The BIG-FIVE factor structure. Journal of Personality and Social Psychology, Vol 59(6) 1216-1229.

Goleman Daniel. 1998.
Working with emotional intelligence. New York: Bantam Books Greenwood, R and Suddaby, R. 2006. Institutional Entrepreneurship

House of Lords Science and Technology Select Committee, 2011
Behavioural Change Report 1-111

HM Treasury. 2010.
Simple Financial Products, a consultation. 1-21.

HM Treasury. 2011.
A New Approach to Financial regulation. 1-413.

Mature Fields: The Big Five Accounting Firms.
Academy of Management Journal. Vol 49, No 1, 27-48.

Harding Ford. 1994
Rainmaking. Adams Media. 1-287.

Ivyenger Sheena, Lepper Mark, 2000.
Journal of Personality and Social Psychology, Vol (79).

Lipper, Thomson Reuters. 2009.
White Paper. Review of UK fund fees.

MacLeod, D and Clarke, N. 2009.
Engaging for Success: Enhancing Performance Through Employee Engagement. A Report to the Government. 12-157.

Maister David, Green Charles, Galford Robert, 2000.
The Trusted Adviser, Free Press (New York)

Maslow, Abraham H.
A Theory of Human Motivation Psychological Review 50(4) (1943): 370-96.

Meyer, J and Rowan B. 1977.
Institutionalised Organisations: Formal Structure as Myth and Ceremony. The American Journal of Sociology. Vol 83, No 2, 340-363.

Miller and Heiman. Strategic Selling

Mosakowski, E. 1998.
    Entrepreneurial Resources, Organisational Choices and Competitive Outcomes. Organisational Science.
    Vol 9, No 6, 625-643.

Nahphet, J and Sumantra, G. 1998.
    Social Capital, Intellectual Capital and the Organisational Advantage. Academy of Management Review.
    Vol 23, No 2, 242-286.

Oxera. 2009.
    Retail Distribution Review proposals: Impact on market structure and competition. 1-58

Pfeffer, J. 1991.
    Organisational Theory and Structural Perspectives on Management. Journal of Management.
    Vol 17, No 4, 789-803.

Porter, M. E. and M. R. Kramer. 2006.
    Strategy and Society: The Link Between Competitive Advantage and Corporate Social Responsibility. Harvard Business Review 84, no.12: 78–92.

Rackham Neil. Spin Selling McGraw-Hill. 1988. 1-197.

Ross, L. (1991):
    The person and the situation; Perspectives of social psychology: New York; McGraw-Hill

Rotter, J. B. 1954.
    Social learning and clinical psychology.
    New York: Prentice Hall.

Rousseau Denise M. 2005.
    Is There Such A Thing As "Evidence Based Management". Academy of Management Review. Vol31, No 2. 256-269.

Seligman, M. M.E.P 1975.
    Helplessness: on depression, development and death

Senge, P. 1990.
    The Fifth Discipline: The Art and Practice of the Learning Organisation. The Fifth Discipline, Random House Inc. 484-491.

Thaler Richard H and Sunstein Cass R. 2009.
Nudge, Improving decisions about health, wealth and happiness. Penguin Books. 1-295.

Thorenson Otto. 2008
Thorenson Review of generic financial advice: final report. 1-98.

Zucker, L. 1989.
Combining Institutional Theory and Population Ecology: No Legitimacy, No History. American Sociological Review. Vol 54, No 4, 542-545.

Which? Magazine The Money Maze. 2009, 1-13.

Lightning Source UK Ltd.
Milton Keynes UK
UKOW051937150712

196025UK00005B/70/P